The Professional Service Firm

The Professional Service Firm

The Manager's Guide to Maximising Profit and Value

MARK C. SCOTT

With best wishes,

JOHN WILEY & SONS, LTD

Chichester · New York · Weinheim · Brisbane · Singapore · Toronto

Paperback edition 2001

This book was originally published in hardback under the title 'The Intellect Industry.'

Copyright © 1998 by   John Wiley & Sons Ltd,
Baffins Lane, Chichester,
West Sussex PO19 1UD, England

National   01243 779777
International (+44) 1243 779777
e-mail (for orders and customer service enquiries):
cs-books@wiley.co.uk
Visit our Home Page on http://www.wiley.co.uk
or http://www.wiley.com

Other Wiley Editorial Offices

John Wiley & Sons, Inc., 605 Third Avenue,
New York, NY 10158–0012, USA

WILEY-VCH Verlag GmbH, Pappelallee 3,
D-69469 Weinheim, Germany

Jacaranda Wiley Ltd, 33 Park Road, Milton,
Queensland 4064, Australia

John Wiley & Sons (Asia) Pte Ltd, 2 Clementi Loop #02–01,
Jin Xing Distripark, Singapore 129809

John Wiley & Sons (Canada) Ltd, 22 Worcester Road,
Rexdale, Ontario M9W 1L1, Canada

Library of Congress Cataloging-in-Publication Data

A catalogue record of this book is available from the Library of Congress

British Library Cataloguing in Publication Data

A catalogue record for this book is available from the British Library

ISBN 0-471-49948-X

Typeset in 11/13pt Palatino by Vision Typesetting, Manchester
Printed and bound in Great Britain by Biddles Limited, Guildford and King's Lynn.

This book is printed on acid-free paper responsibly manufactured from sustainable forestry,
in which at least two trees are planted for each one used for paper production.

For my sweet wife

Contents

Preface

The professional services industry is such a broad one—ranging from legal advisory through to direct marketing—that it is impossible to do justice to the individual sectors of activity that make it up. Fortunately, the same issues and economic challenges are broadly common to all professional service firms and, hence, the methods of analysis covered in this book can be applied to virtually all areas of the industry, from the investment banking boutiques through to advertising agencies. At heart, the professional services industry is about two things—managing professional talent and managing client relationships. Success is driven by management and mastery of intangibles such as time, professional egos and collective knowledge. In a business world where the premium is increasingly on differentiation through leveraging of people skills and corporate knowledge, the best PSFs are at the cutting edge of industry.

This book is intended to help owners and managers of Professional Service Firms understand the strategic options they face and how to optimize the financial performance of their businesses. It is also intended to help investors understand the immense and underexploited opportunities the industry holds for achieving superior returns. Finally, it is written with the aim of bringing to the attention of managers of manufacturing and service businesses how they might emulate the strategies of Professional Service Firms to enhance their own competitiveness.

This book has been written based on a diverse experience of all types of professional service firms. I owe a debt of gratitude in particular to the many outstanding managers at WPP Group plc's various operating companies who, over a number of years, have helped me understand the intricate issues they face and techniques for securing competitive advantage. Most notably I wish to thank Martin Sorrell for his patient mentoring over the years. I also wish to thank Jon Mostyn of Hill & Knowlton for his excellent insights and Dr Jürgen Ladendorf for his invaluable input. I also owe thanks to my wife for her patience over many weekends spent clattering on the keyboard with the sun shining outside.

About the Author

Mark Coleridge Scott is Executive Vice President of Lake Capital Management, a principal investment group specialising in investing in professional service firms. He formerly held the same position at Lighthouse Global Network, a global marketing services group which was acquired by Cordiant Communications Group plc in August 2000. He was previously Operations Director at WPP Group plc and prior to this worked for a number of years as a management consultant in Europe and the USA. He received his MBA from Harvard Business School and was educated at Oxford and Cambridge Universities. He is the author of *Value Drivers* and *Reinspiring the Corporation*.

Introduction

The professional services industry is not usually thought of as an industry at all. It is usually dismissed as a ragbag of asset-less firms employing unmanageable primadonnas. Few professional service firms are quoted on international markets. It is not an industry which is subjected to much market analysis. You would be hard pressed to find reliable statistics about the key areas of the industry, from advertising through to investment banking. The few firms that get covered by analysts tend to be blended into larger sectors. The quoted advertising agencies, for example, get lumped in with general media firms even though it is a fundamentally different business. There are virtually no market research reports on major sectors of the professional services industry and even basic numbers are not available on the standard company information databases. This so-called industry is one big blur of obfuscation and obscurity. All that can be said about it by most observers is that it is broadly identifiable as a collection of people businesses.

So why give it much thought? Simple. Size and growth! The professional services industry accounts for approximately 17% of all employment in the mature markets of Europe and the USA[1]. In total it had revenues of about $700 billion worldwide in 1997, with growth around 15% per annum[2]. Not only has the

---

[1] OECD database, Paris.
[2] In the professional services industry revenues are different from billings. Billings include the cost of collateral bought on behalf of a client. For example, on a billings basis the marketing services industry alone is around $800 billion.

growth of professional services been dramatic but it continues to drive at rates far in excess of the general rate of GDP growth in the mature economies. The consulting sector, for one, projects ongoing growth at 20% through the next ten years off an estimated base of $60 billion in 1997. Some of the better-known firms, from McKinsey in management consulting through to Goldman Sachs in investment banking, have quietly evolved to become some of the most influential institutions on the planet.

Professional services cover a vast territory of activities, from advertising through to legal work and software consulting. These different markets tend to vary dramatically in terms of their competitive dynamics, as does the structure of the firms competing in them. However, all PSFs[3] are united by one common characteristic—their assets walk out of the front door every evening and their livelihood is founded on fragile client relationships. Like the film business, their key competence is the management of talent. They therefore share a similar set of imperatives—the need to hire, train and motivate a set of talented individuals in order to foster and maintain good relationships with their clients. Their basis of competitiveness is starkly simple— how clever are your people?

Given the size and importance of the professional services industry, the absence of interest shown in it by the academic and consulting community is extraordinary. The industry has yet to be subjected to the same level of scrutiny as almost any industrial sector you care to mention. Despite its absolute growth, it should not therefore be surprising that the PSF industry has shown one of the lowest rates of productivity improvement over the past decade.

What is even more surprising is that the vast and high-quality investment opportunity this sector represents has also been largely overlooked by the financial community. The PSF industry is characterized by high margins, high growth and impressive free cash flow generation—a recipe that would get investors salivating in almost any asset-based business. But this has strangely not been the case with professional services, with one novel exception- Internet service and research firms where the pendulum has swung to the opposite extreme. The PSF industry

---

[3] PSF = professional service firm.

is a diamond so large that everyone seems to have overlooked it!

This book is written for those people who want to understand how to maximize returns from professional services, either as investors, proprietors or managers. Because little consulting or academic attention has been given to PSFs, the level of scrutiny to which most PSFs subject their own operations is also low. Most professional service firms have plenty of margin for improvement. TQM, process analysis and strategic analysis are fairly alien concepts for PSFs. Because of the lack of information and the prevalence of self-financing, the role of venture capital and other financial investors in the professional services area is also low. The balance sheets of PSFs are largely virgin territory for the corporate finance community!

As a result, the professional services market holds great opportunities for shareholders as they strive to improve the efficiency of their operations and hence their ability to generate free cash flow. It also represents a great opportunity for financial investors as long as the risks and opportunities are properly understood. The objective of this short book is to expose the value potential of the PSF industry and flesh out strategies for how it can be tapped.

There is also a benefit to be gained from PSFs for firms and managers who have no intention of getting involved in the industry. Most industrial firms have plenty to learn from professional service organizations. Professional service firms tend to do two things outstandingly well: the first is to hire, train and maintain high-calibre minds; the second is to share collective knowledge at high speed and with great efficiency. In the world economy of the next millennium it is these two skills which will be the primary competitive differentiators in almost all industries. PSFs are also masters of customization and relationship marketing. As the mass-market paradigm which has dominated thinking for the past century gives way to customer responsiveness and targeting, all industrials have a lot to learn from the small firms to which they usually delegate this responsibility and who have refined it over time to an art form. The PSF is the model of the firm of the future; that is why even firms as powerful as IBM are pouring resource into developing their consulting arm rather than focusing solely on manufacturing. Most firms will gradually become more like PSFs.

1
The Inexorable Rise of the Professional Service Firm

PSFs have shown spectacular growth over the past ten years. They are positioned not only to continue growing but also to increase their value added.

What were traditionally viewed as a collection of peripheral service providers have become a vital part of the value chain of most industrial corporations. PSFs have come to perform the thinking and creative function of most client firms. Who designs the corporate identity of the firm? Who advises the firm on which areas of activity to pursue and which to shed? Who decides on the pricing of acquisitions? Who produces the advertising and point of sale material that persuade consumers to buy? Who supplies the data about what customers think about the company's products? Who manages the company's interface with the press? Who manages the firm's communications with its own employees? Who ensures that it is minimizing tax exposures? Part of the glue holding many large industrial organizations together is a collection of independent suppliers providing specialized skills, from investment banks through to design consultancies. That is why PSFs are able to achieve such comparatively high margins.

So why don't clients do these things themselves if they're so important? Because independent PSF specialists can usually do them better. Most larger organizations have tried their hand at in-house support services, from advertising to corporate finance, and most (although not all) have found that they can't do the single most important thing right: attract and retain the highest-calibre professionals. It comes down to a simple fact of human nature; if you're bright it's boring to work on one project. It's far more stimulating to see a wide range of client problems and operate with the objectivity and respect granted by being a professional service supplier rather than a permanent employee of the client. Ultimately you can tell them what they don't want to hear and get away with it!

As a result, the structural ability of most client organizations to attract and maintain talent tends to be far inferior to specialist service suppliers. The dominant flow of people talent is from clients to service suppliers as professional firms hire away smart client individuals to institutionalize their relationships. Once set in motion this cycle has proven hard or even impossible to reverse. The PSF supplier will accrue a degree of specialism and knowledge about a client which will enable it to sustain high prices. In turn it will be able to grant salary levels which the client organization is totally unable to match. As a result the virtuous imbalance of skills will enable prices to be held up and the migration of talent to continue until clients are completely dependent on their PSFs to help them differentiate themselves in their markets.

The widespread shift among industrial clients to a strategy of focusing on core competencies over the past five years has simply acted to increase their dependency on professional service suppliers. Since these functions tend not to be as refined within client organizations as they are within specialist PSFs, they tend to be represented internally by middle management gatekeepers and not regarded as core. Gatekeepers have been the principal focus of attrition for the past ten years. The result has been a hollowing out of many companies—the dominant model is an apple core of a slimmed-down decision-making elite at the top and a slab of functionaries at the bottom. Consequently, the process of converting strategy into market-facing actions through advertising, design or acquisition, etc. tends to be a subcontracted set of functions.

The interesting thing is that this implies a transfer of value added and talent out of most industrial and service organizations and into PSFs. And this is precisely what has happened. The massive growth in the billings of the professional services industry over the past decade has not been totally incremental. It has also been cut out of the hide of industrial and non-professional service firms. Because so much of this PSF activity is in private hands, the shift of shareholder value into this area of the economy has been by stealth, largely unnoticed by analysts and untapped by the financial markets.

The fact that this trend has gone largely unnoticed is more surprising still given that the professional service industry is positioned to develop over the next decade at an even faster rate than it has over the past decade. PSFs have it where it matters.

First, it is now generally accepted that the most valuable asset the third-millennium firm will possess is knowledge, and the core differentiating skill will be the ability to deploy that knowledge to competitive advantage. The ability of most PSFs to manage their collective intellectual assets tends to be far superior to that of their industrial counterparts. While industrials are increasingly relying on management information systems (or MIS) to share knowledge, usually with disappointing results, the process and ethic of knowledge share in PSFs tends to be ingrained in their culture rather than dependent on IT. Most share ideas rapidly and place the sharing of information at the top of the list of professional responsibilities in a way that few industrial or service organizations ever do. Given that what they are selling to their clients is knowledge, this is hardly surprising. The ability of PSFs to attract the best minds means that their knowledge asset base is always being upgraded and their willingness to train means that this knowledge can quickly be leveraged profitably. The value of their collective intellectual assets is going in only one direction!

Second, PSFs can align the interests of the firm and those of the employee with far greater efficiency than a typical industrial firm. Since most employees in PSFs are client facing and their influence on the bottom line can be reasonably measured, it is possible to base rewards on the firm's economic performance with far greater precision than in an industrial concern where employees are functionally specialized. This means that PSFs can respond effectively to the ever greater mobility of skilled labour. By simulating the benefits of being an equity partner, they can replicate the benefits of self-employment while reaping the scale advantages and market presence of a large firm. In a decade where skills will be the primary driver of a firm's ability to differentiate itself and compete, and where such skills will be a finite commodity, PSFs are excellently placed to capitalize on this asset. They will effectively monopolize an increasing share of international brain power.

Third, PSFs are able to benefit fully from all the developments in networked IT, one of the primary drivers of business change. Their primary material is knowledge in the form of research, presentations, case histories and methodologies, all of which are ideally suited to management over client–server networks. The advent of intranets and extranets has allowed PSFs to become even more creative in managing their core asset and deploying knowledge to win client business. It should not therefore be surprising that concepts such as "hot-desking" and "hotelling"[1] originated from the professional service industry. The flexibility of working patterns this fosters has made service firms far better environments for the rising star of the workforce, the working mother—highly educated, adaptable, personable, and underutilized.

THE SCEPTICAL INVESTOR

Yet despite the fact that the PSF sector in general is well positioned to ride the wave of the future, it is not widely viewed as a good investment opportunity. There are several reasons, some of which are defensible, others irrational.

First, there has historically been a lot of suspicion about the quality of PSF earnings, even among quoted professional service firms. Client relationships are believed to be fickle and too dependent on key personnel. Instances such as the collapse of GGT, the quoted UK advertising concern, after the defection of Procter & Gamble as a client stick firmly in the memory. They are also felt to be disproportionately vulnerable to shifts in the economic cycle. The prevailing (and to some degree correct) view is that the first thing that clients cut are their external suppliers, particularly as most PSF activity is associated with one form or another of growth-related objective. In addition, PSFs are usually regarded

---

[1] Hotelling is a system whereby professionals book into desks rather than have permanently assigned desks. Hotelling strategies are dependent on efficient IT networks. We will explore the efficiencies this implies in Chapter 7.

as not being rigorously financially controlled, with creative and analytical maniacs holding free sway without any consideration of cost control.

In fact, the quality of earnings of most professional service firms is as high or sometimes higher than their industrial counterparts. Business is based typically on close personal contacts, mutual trust and the collective reputation of the firm. These client relationships tend to be quite enduring.[2] Contracts are seldom based on price as a principal purchase criterion, in contrast to most mature industrial and service segments. This means that key revenue sources tend to be more defensible and to carry higher margins. Most professional service contracts are also characterized by bonuses for performance, which closely links the interests of the client and the PSF. Combined with low fixed costs and capital expenditure, the net effect of these characteristics is to give the PSF industry an excellent ability to convert revenue into free cash flow.

The impression that professional service firms are vulnerable to the whims of one or two brains on legs that can walk is also usually overstated in the case of medium-sized and larger firms. The intellectual assets of a firm tend to be embodied in the collective knowledge of the firm and its culture rather than solely in a number of individuals. The tangible expression of this is the corporate brand. The brands associated with professional service firms are valuable guarantees of quality in exactly the same way as consumer brands. Larger service firms such as Arthur Andersen have even gone so far as to become heavy advertisers. The McKinsey brand carries almost a cult status of prestige and intellectual superiority in the consulting industry. Acquisitive firms pay large multiples of net asset value in the form of goodwill for target PSFs because of the future earnings potential of strong professional service brands. In an industry of intangibles, the brand represents a point of tangible reassurance. In the smart firms it is the culture not just the individuals that embody the reputation of the firm.

Longevity is one of the most admired qualities of major industrial firms[3]. The usual assumption is that professional service

---

[2] As one example, J. Walter Thompson, the advertising agency, has been servicing Unilever for over half a century.
[3] See *Built to Last*, by Porass and Collins. See Select Bibliography.

firms spring up and disappear as fast as dawn mushrooms. In fact, there are as many venerable PSFs as there are industrials. J. Walter Thompson, for one has, just celebrated its 130th birthday. Merrill Lynch, the investment bank, can trace its roots back to 1885. Baker & McKenzie, the world's largest law firm, first opened its doors in 1949.

Longevity can, of course, disguise lack of change and renewal. The life cycle of the technologies underpinning most large PSFs is far longer than those of the average industrial concern. The basic process surrounding the production of a piece of TV advertising hasn't changed for thirty years. Audits are conducted in much the same way as they were fifty years ago. The basis for valuing companies has not altered substantively for ten years since the advent of DCFs. Most professionals organize their work processes in the same way they did half a century ago. By contrast, most manufacturing processes and the products they produce have changed beyond all recognition over the past twenty years. Given this, it is extraordinary that the PSF sector has managed to sustain such spectacular growth. The reason is simple—their brands go through perpetual dynamic renewal as generation after generation of smart people join the firm.

Contrary to common opinion, PSFs are in fact quite financially nimble despite a lesser focus on cost control than their industrial counterparts. Most are able to shed costs rapidly and flexibly in periods of revenue downturn. This means that they can defend their margins even without growth. Industrial firms, by comparison, are typically lumbered with far greater fixed costs, which are not easily removed without lumpy reductions in capacity. Capital expenditure in PSFs is only a fraction of that of industrials and depreciation is often negligible. The only real fixed cost, the rental and ancillary costs of the building, should not typically exceed 10–12% of revenues. This means that even in a revenue downturn a PSF can continue to convert a high percentage of revenue to free cash flow in a way that no industrial could contemplate. The result is that the volatility of earnings can actually be lower in professional service firms than industrials if they are well managed. This can offset the vulnerability of many professional service segments to shifts in the underlying economy. (If, the first thing that industrials shed in periods of downturn is their expenditure on external services, they are also the first thing they spend on when revenues pick up!)

So why do people attribute high systematic risk to professional service firms as investment targets? One reason is quite simply that there is not a great deal of collective experience of investing in them. The historical need of PSFs for capital has not been great. On the whole a smaller PSF can manage its work in progress or WIP (their counterpart of inventory) and working capital sufficiently to fund growth. This is slowly beginning to change. Over the past ten years a large number of private companies have come to the market, primarily to raise capital to acquire competitors and form global networks. As the pressure for professional service firms to globalize increases, for the first time there is a compelling need for external capital to fund expansion and acquisitions. Retained earnings are no longer enough to sustain the speed of growth required to remain competitive. As the volume of deals and listings increases, the level of understanding and comfort investors have with people businesses will also increase.

So why bother with this disparate, fragmented sector as an investor. Because it is high growth, its share of industrial value added will continue to grow even faster, and the risks are comparatively low. The question is how to invest sensibly and how to extract maximum value from the PSF both as an investor and a manager. In most cases there are plenty of additional margin points to be extracted! We have not yet seen productivity improvements among PSFs of the magnitude seen in industry. This simply means that there is a lot of potential in the sector for a major boost in underlying productivity to add to the heady top-line growth—a golden combination!

LEARNING FROM PSFs

Another reason to pay attention to the PSF sector is to learn something about the shape of the organization of the future. The PSF sector is almost never considered when academics and consultants are citing best practice or establishing performance benchmarks. Instead, there is always the same array of industrials, consumer package goods and service businesses. In fact, the PSF industry holds many lessons for all other areas of industry as all firms move into the information economy. Why? Because PSFs do a number of things better than any other type of firm; namely they attract, train and motivate highly intelligent young people and garner, package and share knowledge with great efficiency. PSFs are also masters of customization and have to remain perpetually creative and innovative in their approach to providing client service.

The great challenge for the majority of firms in the West over the next decade will be how to build competitive advantage through the quality of their people and the quality of their collective knowledge. Reliance on privileged market access and access to capital are almost gone as sources of competitive advantage. So too is the ability of Western firms to chase low-cost strategies and to rely on mass marketing. The only option left is to differentiate, to customize and to maintain premiums through perpetual innovation, extremely sharp market focus and an array of intangibles such as branding, aftersales service and market strategy.

In virtually all markets the firms that have done this best are the PSFs. The PSF industry is also an area in which the best performers are almost exclusively Western players. McKinsey is the most prestigious hirer in most international markets for economics graduates. J. Walter Thompson, McCann-Erickson, Ogilvy & Mather and Young & Rubicam remain a foremost aspiration for arts graduates in many international markets. The likes of Andersen Consulting continue to push into newly developing markets, competing successfully for the best talent. Even in Japan the international professional service providers such as Goldman Sachs and Merrill Lynch are becoming competitive hirers of premier graduates. By comparison, many industrials are having an increasingly hard time hiring and hanging onto the best people. Why work for a client when you can earn 50% more in a PSF, get exposure to many different clients and travel the world? This means the knowledge base of many industrials is comparatively in decline and, along with it, their ability to differentiate. This is also why the PSF sector has been growing at such a clip at a time of increasing skill shortages.

At a time when most western industrials are confronting a major cost disadvantage compared to Far Eastern manufacturers and a lower rate of investment, the PSF industry is continuing to build a skills advantage *vis-à-vis* the tiger economies and sustaining a domestic growth rate in the double digits.

2
Segmenting the Professional Services Industry

"Professional Services" is a generic name for a large number of sectors and not just one. There are seven key professional service sectors which probably account for approximately 75% of the entire industry on a revenue basis, with the remaining 25% composed of a disparate collection of activities through from talent agents to architects' practices (Figure 2.1 (a))[1]:

- Investment banking services
- Audit, tax and accountancy advisory services
- Commercial legal advisory services
- Marketing communications services
- Management and IT consulting services
- Recruitment, placement and personnel services
- Market research services

Each key sector can in turn be broken down into a large number of segments (Figure 2.1 (b) illustrates their approximate size and key constituent parts). While in aggregate the key sectors have been growing at a fair clip, each major area of the professional services industry divides into mature segments and high-growth segments with very different characteristics. Audit, for example, is mature and competition is beginning to revert to price. As a result the Big Six accountancy firms (shortly to become the Big

---

[1] Since most PSFs are in private hands, there are scant figures available for the entire PSF industry. The figures in this book are best estimates based on a wide number of industry sources.

Five due to the proposed merger of Coopers & Lybrand with Price Waterhouse) have all aggressively diversified into the high-growth segments of due diligence and corporate finance advisory. Advertising is similarly maturing as an industry and the longevity of client relationships falling, promoting a shift to price as a major purchase criterion. By contrast, the area of direct marketing, focused on customer targeting, is showing high levels of growth particularly in database applications. Internet-related communications, an offshoot of direct marketing, is simply going ballistic.

Professional services, just like consumer products, demonstrate a steady migration from mature products to new products or segments. As segments mature they tend to experience a process of industry consolidation as rivals compete for a finite number of global client accounts. Both the advertising industry and the accounting industry have seen a steady process of consolidation of major activities into the hands of a small number of global players: 57% of the world's advertising spend is concentrated in the hands of ten agencies, up from 46% in 1983. In the case of accountancy, which is even further down the maturity curve, the C6/C5 ratio is around 50%[2]. By contrast, high growth segments tend to be highly fragmented, made up of a plethora of innovative private PSFs. The Internet field, for example, is a web of tiny "hot-shops". The employee communications business is a sprawl of one-man advisors. Figure 2.2 illustrates the level of maturity of some of the key segments of the major sectors of the professional services industry.

CONSOLIDATION VERSUS SPECIALIZATION

At one extreme of the PSF spectrum are the highly consolidated segments dominated by global networks. The consolidation of PSF segments tends to closely track the globalization of client firms and the shift of economic activity away from the mature economies. As clients begin to push global products and services, so PSFs tend to consolidate behind them. Often the most highly consolidated service areas are those in which the client reaps

---

[2] A C6 ratio is the collective market share represented by the top six players.

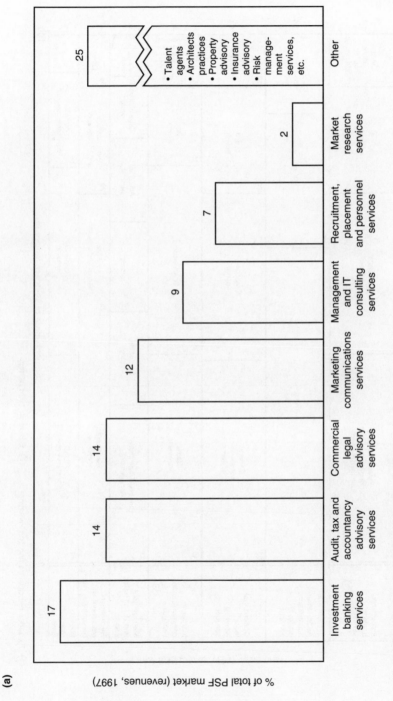

Figure 2.1(a) Approximate share of global PSF industry of key PSF sectors

(b)

% of total PSF market (1997 revenues)

			Segment share of sector revenues (%) →		
Investment banking services ①	40 Sales, trading, broking services and fund management	30 Corporate finance	20 M & A advisory	10 Other (venture capital/ private equity)	17
Audit, tax and accountancy advisory services	60 Auditing	25 Corporate finance	15 Corporate finance related		14
Commercial legal advisory services	38 General commercial advisory	32 Corporate finance	20 M & A activity	10 Other	14
Marketing communications services ②	40 Sales promotion	35 Advertising	15 Direct mail	5 Design and identity · 5 Other (internet marketing services)	12
Management and IT consulting services	31 Process/IT/operations management	17 Corporate strategy · 17 IT strategy	16 Actuarial/ benefits · 11 Organizational design	6 Financial advisory · 2 Marketing and sales	9
Recruitment, placement and personnel services	45 Placement services	25 Ad hoc search and selection	20 Remuneration and HR advisory	10 Other	7
Market research services	40 Ad hoc quantitative research	35 Continuous research	18 Ad hoc qualitative research	7 Regular tracking	2

0 — Segment share of sector revenues (%) — 100

① Excludes principal trading and investing ② Based on 1994 billings

Figure 2.1(b) Approximate composition of key PSF sectors

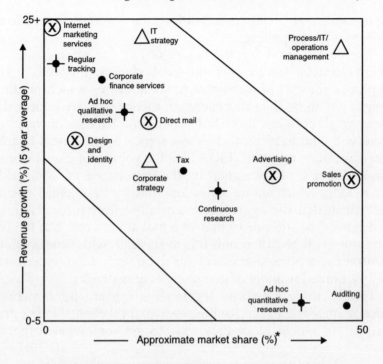

Figure 2.2 Simplified illustration of maturity of selected PSF segments

benefits from economies of scale. Advertising copy that can be shared globally or an audit which can easily be consolidated both offer the client decisive advantages. Of course, since they have few fixed costs, most service firms do not enjoy substantial economies of scale so the benefit is not always shared by the PSF. The advertising agency and the auditing firm still have to service the client locally as well as globally and, although they may have one name and a set of networked offices, the economies of scale are not usually compelling.

The next stage down the ladder of PSF evolution is the segment characterized by the multi-local network (Figure 2.3). This typically consists of a chain of national offices which might or might not share the same name. In theory they are expected to refer work between them but usually the balance of the client base will tend to be local. This is a typical arrangement in areas such as public relations (PR) where the volume of global work is limited and far outweighed by the importance of local media knowledge which has no scale economies for the client. This does not mean that the aggregate financial performance of the network need be inferior to that of a global network, but the cost structure will be different if it is to succeed, with little room for central costs. Such segments tend to be fairly fragmented, with only a limited number of genuine global networks.

Finally, there are those segments which are fundamentally local, competing to service the needs of local clients. In the great scuffle for global glory they tend to get somewhat forgotten.

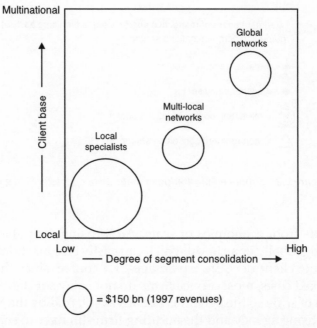

Figure 2.3 *Approximate relative position of generic PSF segment clusters*

However, they still constitute the bulk of PSF activity. They are also the domain of the "rising star" and often typified by firms with the highest growth rates as they move to develop multi-local networks.

The evolution of professional services in one direction only—consolidation—is not unchallenged. It has been matched by increasing specialization. In all areas of marketing services there has been a growth in targeted specialists, often as breakaways from less focused and larger parent companies. In the world of consulting, for example, firms such as McKinsey have been the breeding ground for a number of sector-focused strategy firms. The same is true of research, particularly in areas such as IT and Internet-focused research where firms such as Forrester, Gartner and Meta have a dominant position. PR similarly has incubated a number of sector-focused powerhouses, particularly in the areas of finance and healthcare such as Dewe Rogerson.

Many of the consolidated global professional service groups are no more than a collection of a diverse group of highly specialist firms who may or may not chose to work with each other depending on the client situation. The individual companies within these groups are often highly competitive with each other. Omnicom, IPG and WPP, who dominate the marketing services sector, each own specialist agencies which compete head to head with each other. Andersen Consulting and Arthur Andersen Consulting, for example, appear to view each other as mortal enemies. In a paradoxical way, the process of specialization is the by-product of the same maturity that also drives consolidation.

Nor are any professional service sectors static. Each segment and sector is always encroaching on the other. The rate of substitution in most areas of professional services has accelerated dramatically over the last ten years. Classical advertising, the incumbent powerhouse with global billings of around $400 billion in 1997, has been losing share to a plethora of direct marketing, database marketing and promotions activities, most of which are delivered by smaller businesses. The growth of Internet-related marketing has simply acted to accelerate this trend. In consulting the rate of innovation is even faster. A firm such as CSC Index came from nowhere on the back of a single innovative concept—Business Process Re-engineering or BPR. The Renaissance Solutions Group is doing the same on the back of The Balanced Scorecard.[3] In a sector where capital is not usually a decisive factor for startups, innovation tends to occur through independent enterprise rather than being controlled by incumbents with capital. Agencies buying into Internet companies are high cost, not attempting to start them themselves. The specialist tends to be a substitute and so is slowly but surely snapped up by its larger cousins, the generalists.

Along with this delicate balance between consolidation and specialization, there is an increasing blurring taking place between the classical distinctions governing professional service segments. Auditing firms are morphing into consulting firms, as well as entering the commercial law and corporate finance sectors. Consulting firms are beginning to encroach on the brand strategy issues traditionally the exclusive domain of the advertising agencies. Recruitment firms have extended into internal communications and marketing work (Figure 2.4).

The fact this is occurring is not exactly surprising. The finite commodity in the market are strong client relationships and, since these are the core assets of PSFs, the easiest means of maximizing income is extending the business done through key clients by providing a "one-stop shop". Professionals are also migrating across service disciplines with increasing speed and transferring disciplines with them, particularly under the umbrellas of holding companies. The result is the continual collapse of simple distinctions between services.

Most PSF segments tend to shift over time to a polarity of a small number of large networks and a large number of smaller innovators and specialists which, as fast as they are acquired and merged, will be replaced by new start-ups with aggressive growth trajectories. Twenty years ago the ratio of major networks to specialists in terms of dollar billings[4] was probably 1:2. Over the next decade this ratio is likely to stabilize at around 1:1 in most professional service segments. The cycle of start-up and acquisition will remain an unusually fast and dynamic one in all PSF sectors.

---

[3] *The Balanced Scorecard* by Kaplan and Norton, See Select Bibliography.
[4] The term "billings" is peculiar to PSFs and will be explored in detail in later chapters.

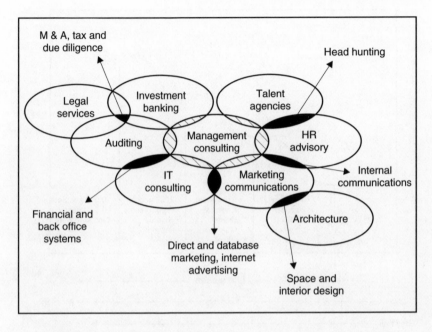

Figure 2.4   *Illustrative examples of convergence in the PSF industry*

LIFE STAGES

Within any given segment PSFs tend to follow the same life stages. The first stage is start-up and early growth up to about $3million in fee income.[5] The firm will have about thirty people in a single office serving a local client base. It will probably be quite dependent on a couple of key clients and one or two business winners. Stage two usually spans fee income from $3million up to around $10million. The firm may have expanded out of a single office. It will certainly have clients on a national or regional basis. It will have a strong local specialist reputation and two or three significant accounts which will tend to be "secure". Stage three runs up to about $50million in fee income. The firm will have a small network of offices based around core regional or international cities. Its reputation will be strong and it will be widely regarded as a mature business, with upwards of 300 employees.

[5] Fee income is real revenue. As we will explore presently, this differs from billings which includes the value of bought-in services.

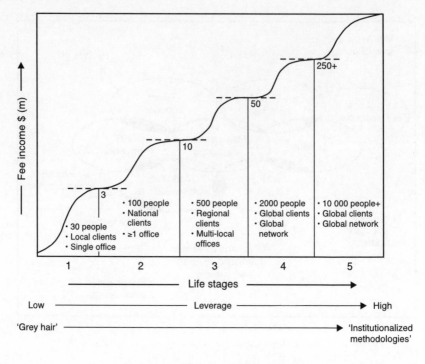

Figure 2.5   *Generic life stages for PSFs*

Stage-four firms will have grown as far as around $250million in fee income. They will typically still be specialized but have a significant network of global offices and be well recognized as an international brand in their segment. They will tend to have gurus and well-known industry figureheads on the board. They may have started to become quite acquisitive and their business will be founded on a number of key global client relationships. They will widely be regarded as being an institutionalized brand, no longer vulnerable to the whims of a small number of managers. Stage-five firms will have income that may stretch into the billions. They will typically be acquisitive and have a holding of PSFs from a potentially wide spectrum of sectors. In any PSF segment there will typically be no more than a handful of such firms. Depending on the level of consolidation in the sector, they are more likely than not to be quoted. Figure 2.5 illustrates the life stages segmentation of PSFs.

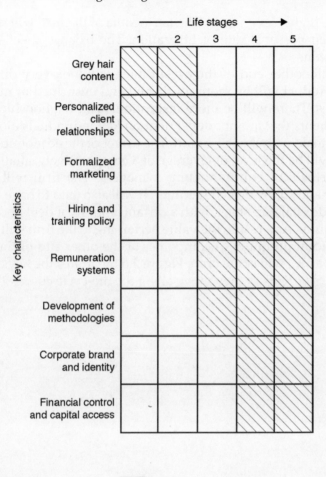

Figure 2.6 *Primary points of management focus in PSFs at different life stages*

Firms at each of these different life stages will face quite distinct problems, opportunities and very different challenges to remain competitive. They will also have evolved fundamentally different ways of operating. At the early end of the life cycle the firm will typically rely on a handful of senior professionals and their close personal client relationships. The product will often have a heavy "grey hair" advisory content and each partner will not be highly leveraged.[6] The fee income of the firm will depend on their personal rate of utilization. The balance sheet will be very thin.

At the other end of the cycle things will look very different. The product will be more routinized and enshrined in methodologies. There will be more institutionalized relationships with key clients that are not dependent on key individuals alone but more to do with the PSF brand. The driver of the economics of the firm will be the level of leverage of a comparatively small group of partners or equity-holding managers. The firm will be an active and sophisticated recruiter. It will also tend to have a more orthodox balance sheet, with a certain amount of debt and external equity. As a result, the value pertaining to the firm will be at a significant premium to companies at the other end of the spectrum, as we will come onto. Figure 2.6 illustrates the key characteristics of PSFs as they move along the life-cycle curve.

---

[6] Leverage is the ratio of partners to employees or business winners to business doers. As we will explore in later chapters, leverage is a major driver of the ability of the PSF to generate fee income.

3
Determining the Relative Attractiveness of Segments of the Professional Services Industry

While all PSFs will obey the basic tenets of the life cycle, the fundamental attractiveness of different segments will vary dramatically, as will the competitive demands placed on protagonists. For a player in any given segment (and also for investors) it is essential to understand the nature of competition and its key drivers. The PSF market model[1] illustrated in Figure 3.1 is a simple way of analysing the nature of competition and therefore the relative attractiveness of different PSF segments in terms of their potential profitability. The PSF market model is composed of six key drivers of the level and type of competition in any PSF segment:

- Growth and cyclicality
- Entry and exit barriers
- Client dependency
- Recruitment and retention patterns
- Threat of service substitution
- Impact of government activity

---

[1] There have been a number of generic industrial market models over the years, the most famous and archetypal of which is Michael Porter's Five Forces. See Select Bibliography.

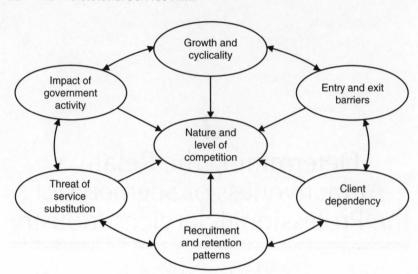

Figure 3.1 *The PSF market model*

NATURE AND LEVEL OF COMPETITION

Most good professional service businesses should achieve operating margins[2] in excess of 20%. This is above most industrial
manufacturers and service providers and reflects the high value
added per professional of PSFs. It also reflects the fact that the
dominant purchase criterion for many segments is not price. The
best services tend to be bought on a value-pricing model reflecting the value of the service to the client, the quality of the
professionals delivering it and the quality of the firm's market
reputation. The "product" will be highly customized. Often the
buyer will be senior management and they will not be price
sensitive. In such situations projects tend not to be put out to
tender but to be awarded on a personal basis.

As you might expect, in professional service sectors where the
basis of competition is on price operating margins will tend to
fall below 20%. Clients will typically hold pitches of multiple
suppliers for contracts and margins will be transparent. The
length of the average client relationship will be short. Typically

---

[2] Operating margin = operating profits over revenues or gross margin, as we will
explore in Chapter 5.

the segment will have witnessed progressive consolidation as competitors attempt to restore margins by redressing the balance of supply with the power of buyers. Often such segments will also be characterized by a high turnover of staff and migration of employees between key firms. In general, the perceived value added by the client will be on the wane and competitors will tend to be viewed as suppliers rather than partners. The auditing and capital markets segments are classic areas where the basis of competition has begun to revert from value added to price and returns have dropped commensurately.

The problem for PSFs competing in a low-value environment is that a low-cost strategy is not a viable one for the PSF. If a firm tries to reduce its staff or its wage bill, its quality of service will immediately fall and with it clients will start defecting. If pricing drops, the only choice for the PSF will be to watch margins fall—and no firm can do that for ever. In general, it is hard for a firm to sustain a differentiation strategy in a segment which is slipping into cost-based competition, unless it is a local niche or specialist player—the fact that thousands of small PSFs achieve handsome returns is testimony to the fact that niche strategies can pay off, even in tough markets.

Segments which have preserved value as the dominant basis of client appeal tend to be differentiated. Differentiation in the world of PSFs does not simply mean having unique products. The products or intellectual methods and frameworks of PSFs are not particularly defensible. After a year of use, if they are successful, they will quickly be copied. Instead, differentiation means the quality of the intellectual capital of the firm—the collective ability of its senior people, embodied in its brand reputation. If a firm is differentiated, it will be smarter than its clients and it will typically only have a few competitor firms who are able to match it. Its client relationships will tend to be at the most senior level where issues of cost are negligible relative to the value of the advice.

Interestingly, the ability to differentiate is not scale-specific in PSFs. It does not tend to disappear as a firm grows, which is the classic problem with industrial firms. At one extreme, strategy consultants have grown to thousands of professionals and maintained their charge-out rates even though their structure of leverage will have shifted during the process of expansion. At the other extreme, sports event marketing has maintained its margins as a result of key players pursuing niche strategies.

Differentiation in the form of intellectual human capital is a barrier to new entrants and just as tough to overcome as most technological barriers such as familiarity with materials or manufacturing technology. A group of smart people working effectively together cannot easily be emulated or reverse engineered, particularly if they cannot be hired away.

The two key drivers of differentiation in PSFs are the quality of people the segment attracts and the quality of client relationships. In any situation where either of these is on the slide, the segment will tend to suffer lower barriers to entry, more dismissive clients shopping on price and declining margins as Figure 3.2 illustrates.

GROWTH AND CYCLICALITY

All PSFs are top-line focused. The objective of almost all CEOs is to increase revenues. This is partly driven by the sheer intestinal

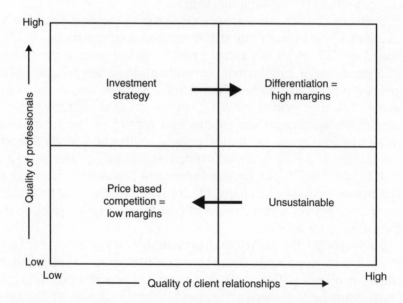

Figure 3.2   *Illustrative relationship between the quality of client relationships, the quality of professionals and profitability*

excitement of winning new pieces of business. As with all businesses, segments which are experiencing high growth leave more room for comfortable expansion without depressing prices. It is when market growth slows and the pains of margin pressure focus the minds of managers on consolidation that competition reverts to a struggle for market share and client share. Growth probably conditions the behaviour of PSFs more than it does industrials because of the unique focus on the revenue line compared to the industrial concern with controlling costs.

Growth itself is largely driven by shifts in the economic cycle and competitive dynamics affecting the spending pattern of PSF clients. This means that much of PSF behaviour is directly driven by what their clients are doing and not by any internal logic. Generally, professional service firms tend to follow the same economic cycle as their clients but with more exaggerated swings between peaks and troughs, for the simple reason that they are in many cases (although not all) the first thing on which cash is spent on upswings and the first to get dumped in downturns. Clearly the more accentuated the response to cyclical swings in the underlying economy, the greater the risk for investors in the business.

There is usually a generic assumption that all PSFs behave the same. In fact, the cyclicality of different segments of the professional service industry differs greatly. The headhunting industry, for example, responds in a very dramatic fashion to recessions and booms, resulting in swings from losses to high profit margins typically over five-year cycles as client firms hire and don't hire. The management consulting industry, by comparison, is able to build in some countercyclical padding by shifting from cost-reduction products such as re-engineering in periods of economic slowdown to revenue-building products such as M&A targeting in periods of growth. Similarly, marketing services firms with capabilities in both advertising and promotions (a great rarity it is worth pointing out!) are able to exploit growth periods where above-the-line[3] spending always picks up, combined with insulation against downturns where promotional activity typically accelerates at the expense of advertising. Investment bankers similarly try to maintain expertise in putting

---

[3] Above-the-line is advertising parlance for pure brand advertising activity as opposed to promotional or direct marketing activity which is classified as below-the-line.

acquisitions together in upturns along with restructurings, un-bundling holdings and performing private placements during downturns.

The cyclicality of different PSF segments is a major drive of the nature of competition in those segments. Since major cyclicality uncouples long-term client relationships and makes it tough for the firm to develop a consistent professional staff base, it tends to push the PSF towards competing on price rather than differenti-ation. When revenues fall away most PSFs will fight to maintain utilization rather than disrupt their professional body by firing people. The only way of doing this is to lower prices and try to maintain volume. The problem is that once pricing expectations have been fundamentally lowered they usually prove very hard indeed to reverse. The result is that the margin potential of the firms in the segment will be fundamentally lowered, unless they are able to alter the underlying leverage in their structure.[4]

While PSFs have a relatively high degree of exposure to cycli-cal volatility, if well managed they actually have the ability to smooth the cycle more efficiently than their clients. The wide-spread process of shedding non-core activities will increasingly limit the ability of most clients to cut back the use of professional service suppliers during periods of slowdown. Hence PSFs should increasingly be in a better position to defend their rev-enues in slowdowns.

Smart PSFs are also able to shift tactically between counter-cyclical products in a way that is not possible for their clients, in essence customizing themselves to shifts in demand. As already discussed, the consultants are the classic case in point, migrating between cost-saving concepts such as re-engineering during re-cessions and marketing-related strategy products during up-turns. The fact that management consultancy has shown a steady 20% growth rate across the economic cycles of the past two decades suggests that PSFs are fully able to smooth out the curve. As far as the next decade goes, the growth potential of most PSF segments would appear great enough to avoid excessive press-ures on pricing.

---

[4] We will come onto the issue of leverage and its impact on profitability in Chapter 6.

ENTRY AND EXIT BARRIERS

It is a common assumption that the entry barriers to most professional services are non-existent. There is, after all, no machinery other than PCs, office space is usually available on short leases, and professional service people tend to arrive university or professionally trained.

Actually, in PSF segments where firms compete successfully based on differentiation there tend to be significant entry barriers. The most important entry barriers, of course, are client relationships and credibility. The major multinational clients are highly guarded by the primary service providers and it is usually tough for a new entrant to replicate the institutionalized nature of a long-term relationship, along with the accumulated knowledge of the client that strong incumbent firms will possess. Major clients with substantial budgets will tend only to move business between the established major service networks and not risk putting their trust in start-up shops. Having said that, segments where the client's purchase criteria have shifted away from value tend to witness diminishing lengths of relationships as "switching costs" fall away. In such situations it is common for large clients to experiment with "hot shops" on the margin both to accommodate highly localized and particular needs and to put pressure on their larger PSF partners.

With smaller accounts it is a different story altogether. It only takes a good rapport between one professional and one client to forge a piece of business. A few of those and the firm is up and running and can fund office space and personnel out of operating cash flow. This means that most PSF segments witness a continual percolation of new brands, often run by old hands that have started and sold previous companies and come to the end of their "earn-outs".[5] Segments dominated by such businesses tend to be subject to price-based competition, as is the case with PR for example.

Entry barriers also exist in the form of the ability of a firm to hire talent and keep it. The quality and depth of talent tends to correlate closely with the ability to win and maintain good clients. The two generic means of building competitive defences go

---

[5] Earn-outs are a particular structure of acquisition involving payment through a set of deferred considerations. We will explore this in detail in Chapter 8.

hand in hand—the good people will migrate to those firms who have good accounts and good accounts will be won by good people. Entry barriers are created by a combination of client value and professional value. The size of entry barriers on this basis will correspond closely with the profits of the key firms in each segment.

The counterpart of entry barriers are exit barriers. If a firm is losing money and unable to exit it will tend to drag down the pricing in a segment as it fights to maintain capacity utilization. While exit barriers are a major issue in many industrial segments, affecting the pricing and therefore profitability of all players, they are not an issue for most PSFs. The simple reason is capital. Industrials have to take a major hit to close a factory or production line and will battle to exceed break-even to the death. PSFs can ultimately fire everybody except the partners with relatively minimal costs necessary to fulfil employment contracts (a few countries such as Germany and Japan being the exception). If a PSF is losing money for a couple of years it will typically fundamentally restructure its cost base and scale back. The result is that a single sector or segment is unlikely to be dragged down by a few losing firms.

CLIENT DEPENDENCY

With consolidation among the major clients occurring faster than among advisory suppliers, most PSF segments have experienced an increasing imbalance of power between suppliers and buyers. The primary expression of purchasing power is either to lower price or to demand levels of resource which are not profitable for the PSF to provide. This means a gradual erosion of margins. The relative degree of consolidation is not, however, the sole driver of negotiating power. The key is the ability of the firm to be valued by its clients. A client that values a PSF will tend to accept a "value billing"[6] concept which will make it easier for the PSF to generate high profits. In essence, the purchase criterion will not refer to price in any significant

---

[6] Value billing is a pricing mechanism which relates the payment to the value of the services to the client and not to the costs of delivery for the PSF. We will explore pricing strategies in Chapter 7.

way and the client will not exercise its purchasing power. A client that regards its PSFs as suppliers only will place far greater emphasis on price and it will tend to use its relative strength to negotiate on price. This might involve putting every project out to pitch and maintaining relationships only on a project-by-project basis.

As with any relationship, the easiest way to get a client to value a PSF's services is to make it feel privileged to have access to such brainpower. In a marketplace with consolidation working against it, the only realistic way for a PSF to be coveted is to be a high-class whore. The problem in many PSF segments is that this is not easy to do. At one extreme, advertising industry norms make it practically impossible for an agency to work for two clients in the same industry without losing the business of one of them through "conflict". While the principle of "no conflicts" would imply beneficial partnership, the balance of power between the buyer and the supplier in this situation is radically skewed in favour of the client, with obvious results.

At the other extreme, the management consulting firms such as McKinsey appear to be able both to service multiple clients in the same sector and to maintain absolutely premium billing rates. In certain sectors such as banking McKinsey appears to have a relationship with virtually all the major players. The effect is to swing the balance of power almost entirely in their favour. In general, PSF sectors where relationships are exclusive tend, almost counterintuitively, to be lower margin. Of course, the trade-off with monogamy is a secure income stream which allows for investment and lower systematic risk for investors.

The growing trend among the successful management consulting firms is for sector specialization. This is for the simple reason that it offers far greater opportunity to counteract the corrosive effects of single client dependency. Deeper knowledge can be developed about a sector than is available to any single client. The PSF becomes the conduit of information between players and entry barriers can be established. The ability of the firm to shift client purchase criteria firmly away from price is greatly enhanced. Sector specialists tend, not surprisingly, to be more profitable than traditional product line specialists as we will come onto.

RECRUITMENT AND RETENTION PATTERNS

The suppliers to PSFs are individuals; either fresh graduates or seasoned professionals. Clearly the imbalance in power between an individual and a company would appear to weigh the negotiation in favour of the firm. This holds true when supply is plentiful. Structurally, however, this is set to change over the coming decade. Historically there has been little constraint on absolute supply with the growth in university graduates and the explosion of professional qualifications such as the ubiquitous MBA. With growth in PSFs far outstripping that of the quality graduating student population, this will no longer hold true in the future. Big Six firms alone have been adding between 5000 and 7000 professionals each a year, almost equivalent to the entire graduating class of Harvard, Yale, Stanford, Oxford and Cambridge combined.

This will have a critical impact on the profitability of most PSFs. Typically PSFs make their highest margins off fresh graduates where the billing rate to salary multiple is by far the highest, combined with the highest rates of utilization in the firm. The absolute rates that are chargeable are not inelastic which means that any inflation in starting salaries will erode margin levels. It is almost certainly the case that wage inflation among graduates is exceeding the growth in average PSF charge-out rates. The result will be that firms competing in predominantly cost-based segments will be unable to pass on costs and be forced to seek productivity gains to combat margin erosion. The value pricing firms will actually do better as clients themselves are unable to hire super-high-quality people and are forced to swallow higher bills as a result in order to keep the services of the best firms.

Competition for experienced people (as opposed to new hires) is already formidable and the ability of such people to switch is increasing. Again, the rate of growth in PSFs is far higher than people can be pushed and promoted organically up the hierarchy. The result is a major shortage of good people in the middle ranks of most PSFs. Competition for middle-ranking professionals and rising stars tends to be ferocious, creating a high salary gap between people with five-plus years' experience and graduates. Again, the firms that can sustain value pricing approaches are the ones who are able to pay the salaries and consolidate the talent.

The net effect of the increasing power of the individual supplier, of course, will be to polarize the PSF market further. The premium firms with the best reputations and training schemes, such as McKinsey, Goldman Sachs or Baker & McKenzie, will strengthen their hold of the best and brightest and harden their margins. Focused smaller players will compete based on the promise of earlier partnership, client exposure and equity. The losers, as usual, will be the medium-sized firms with institutionalized career paths but second-tier brands. The next decade of development in PSFs will be the decade when it will not be good to be stuck in the middle.

PSFs are quite different from their industrial counterparts in the level of impact that the supply side can have on the business. The PSF has to pay as much attention to maintaining and renewing its professional base as it does to winning new clients—they are both sides of the same coin.

THREAT OF SERVICE SUBSTITUTION

Among industrials the source of most substitution is new technology. The typewriter manufacturer is happily pumping out key clackers when the PC industry is born and within five years wipes it out. Technological substitution occurs as often in production technology as it does in end products themselves. A car manufacturer mastering new production line efficiencies can achieve a cost advantage that enables it to price a competitor out of the market. In most industrial sectors the pace of process and product innovation has meant that competitors are continually trying to outflank each other to achieve competitive advantage. Substitution is a continual threat. This means ever higher capex[7] charges with their associated impact on free cash flow and hence risk to the investor.

PSFs do not have technology in the industrial sense of the word. Their work methods and frameworks are easily copied. The only proprietary material possession is the brand at the foot

[7] Capex = capital expenditure.

of the "overheads".[8] Substitution does not occur through the appearance of a more advanced technique; it occurs through competitors making more compelling claims to a client than the incumbent firm. Substitution is simply a continual process of prizing away clients through superior reputation and talent.

This means that the life of the PSF is very different from its industrial counterpart. It does not have to invest in R&D and new productive capital other than IT to keep ahead of the curve. Nor does it have to envision what will be the next turn of the techno-logical road (although it clearly can't ignore it either). What it has to do instead is make sure that its energies are focused on serving the client with maximum effectiveness and that it invests in the professional resource necessary to maintain standards. This means that, instead of diverting resources into non IT capex and suffering increasing depreciation charges against earnings which may or may not translate into cash flow down the road, the PSF can focus all its energies on keeping its clients happy. And happy clients will quickly allow the PSF to convert revenue into free cash flow. All the PSF has to worry about is whether the quality of its service exceeds that offered by its immediate competitors. Substitution is the litmus test of a company losing competitive-ness.

IMPACT OF GOVERNMENT ACTIVITY

Government accounts for around 30–40% of the economic activ-ity of the mature Western economies. It should not therefore be surprising that it is the single largest client for almost all PSFs segments in one guise or other. Most governments are under pressure to shed fixed costs, which simply has the effect of augmenting the demand for PSF providers from the public sec-tor.

The difference between most government departments and private enterprise is that public contracts are usually awarded based on standardized submission of tender. Also, each contract tends to have a finite life before being put out to tender once more. This shifts the basis of purchase from long-term relation-

---

[8] "Overheads" is the pervasive consulting lingo for slide projections used in presentations.

ships and value added to a cost/efficiency equation. The impact of that is, of course, to lower the margins for suppliers because of lower billing rates and the need to amortize the cost of account acquisition over a shorter time period.

Firms and segments which are highly dependent on government contracts are unlikely to have the stability of earnings of ones which focus on private accounts. Therefore, segments which are dominated by public work tend in general to be fundamentally less attractive than those which do not come into contact with government contracts. This observation is often somewhat counter-intuitive because public accounts tend to be very large and prestigious. They will often allow smaller PSFs to double their size instantaneously. Of course, therein lies much of their danger. Large growth in revenues, and hence professional costs, at unattractive margins with little chance of long-term continuity—a recipe for disaster.

PULLING IT ALL TOGETHER

Figure 3.3 illustrates how some of the major PSF segments are likely to fare over the next decade based on an assessment using the PSF market model. Good firms will always make money in any segment, but the message is clear. In the mature segments with declining margins and low differentiation, firms either have to consolidate and win scope and scale economies essential for servicing the ever-larger accounts of global clients or they have to specialize, focus and differentiate. The option of doing nothing is no longer a viable one – medium-sized firms will increasingly be in trouble. The margins for those two sets of competitors should remain healthy and growth rates far above that enjoyed by clients in the majority of industrial segments. In these cases the ability of good firms to convert revenue to free cash flow will far outstrip that of virtually any other business sector.

Growth / Cyclic- ality	Entry and exit barriers	Client depen- dency	Recruitment and retention patterns ✲	Threat of service substitution	Impact of government activity	Nature and level of competition
TV and press advertising — Medium / Medium	Medium	High	Medium	High	Low	High ●
Promotions — Medium / High	Low	Medium	Low	Medium	Low	High ●
Direct mail — High / Medium	Low	Medium	Low	Medium	Low	Medium ◑
Database and relationship marketing — High / Medium	Medium	Low	Medium	Low	Low	Medium/ low ○
Interactive marketing — High / Medium	Low	Low	High	Low	Low	Low/ Medium ○
Audit — Low / Low	High	High	Medium	Low	High	High ●
Tax — Medium / Low	High	Medium	Medium	Low	High	High ◑
Business consulting — High / Medium	Medium	Medium	High	Medium	Medium	Medium/ low ○
Corporate finance — High / Medium	Medium	Low	High	Medium	Medium	Medium ◑

✲ Low = poor

● = cost based competition

○ = differentiation based competition

Figure 3.3 *Illustrative evaluation of market conditions in selected segments of the marketing services and accounting sectors*

4
Generic Strategies for Professional Service Firms

The strategies of PSFs have been driven by one factor more than any other—the strategies of the major clients they service. Most industries have seen a rapid rate of consolidation over the past ten years, combined with a massive push for globalization, either through acquisition or green-field investment in the developing regions. PSFs have dutifully followed the same path, but at a somewhat slower pace and less decisively.

The decisiveness is key. Because both clients and employees can rapidly migrate between PSFs, failure to act can result in the rapid unravelling of a business. Most PSFs have been faced with a real dilemma about how to preserve their differentiation in a market characterized by ever greater degrees of cost-based competition driven by client consolidation. As Figure 4.1 illustrates, PSFs have three key generic axes to choose between in pursuing a strategy:

- Global network versus local, national or regional focus
- Integration or service bundling versus service specialization
- Client sector specialization versus product specialization

Most firms, of course, will follow a blend of all three growth strategies. The issue is how effectively they do so and how much incremental shareholder value is created. The other issue is how firms execute either strategy, whether through acquisition, partnering or organic growth (Figure 4.2).

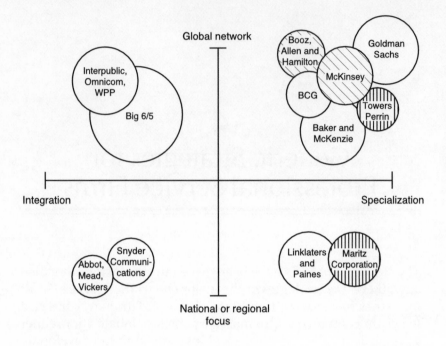

Figure 4.1   *Illustrative generic positioning strategies for PSFs*

GLOBAL SERVICE INTEGRATION OR BUNDLING

As far as industrials are concerned, in the 1960s and 1970s diversified conglomerates were in, along with vertical integration which had emerged in the 1920's. The great beasts such as ITT and Hanson soaked up industries with little in common other than a need for capital. By contrast, the 1990s have all been about focus and specialization. Industrials are continuing to shed "non-core" assets and return to their heartland. This process has

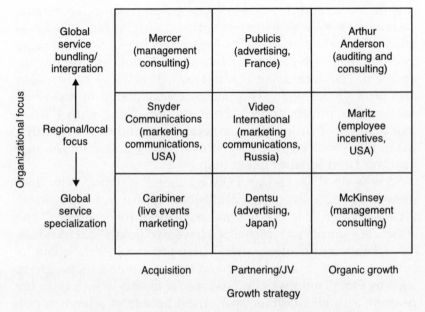

Organizational focus	Acquisition	Partnering/JV	Organic growth
Global service bundling/ intergration	Mercer (management consulting)	Publicis (advertising, France)	Arthur Anderson (auditing and consulting)
Regional/local focus	Snyder Communications (marketing communications, USA)	Video International (marketing communications, Russia)	Maritz (employee incentives, USA)
Global service specialization	Caribiner (live events marketing)	Dentsu (advertising, Japan)	McKinsey (management consulting)

Growth strategy

Figure 4.2 *Illustrative generic growth strategies for PSFs*

been self-perpetuating as the markets now reward firms for following the accepted trend of simplification and punish those who persist in keeping their hands in many pies. Focused players quite simply get higher PEs.[1] This has been accompanied by an increased suspicion of growth that is excessively dependent on acquisition. It is no longer acceptable to grow through unfocused buying sprees. The real stock market rewards are for energetic pursuit of organic growth in the heartland business, possibly supplemented with targeted fill-in acquisitions.

While this logic is inexorable in the traditional industrial and services arena, there is no such compelling dynamic in the PSF sector. In many ways the trend of the larger players has been resolutely in the opposite direction. The rate of merger and acquisition has continued to accelerate from lows in the early 1990s to record heights of consolidation in the late 1990s. The push for pursuing synergies across separate lines of business has been uniform. The Big Six Five are all pushing for growth out-

---

[1] PE = price–earnings multiple calculated by dividing the market value or capitalization of the firm by its average after-tax earnings, or alternatively its share price by its average earnings per share. We will come onto the issue of PEs in detail in Chapter 8.

side their core auditing and tax activities in fields as far-ranging as human resources management, commercial law and back-office systems integration. The investment banks are continuing to extend from advisory work into share dealing and fund management. They are doing this not only in national markets but also on a global scale. The rate of consolidation in most PSF segments continues apace. The interesting thing with PSFs is that this consolidation is across sector lines and not only within them. It is also occurring up and down the value chain through backward and forward integration.

So why do PSFs appear to be bucking the trend? Why does growth through diversified acquisition appear to be acceptable for PSFs when it is not for the majority of other sectors? The reason is a simple one. Most PSFs have two points of commonality—clients and professionals. These are compelling points of synergy. If, for example, a marketing communications group such as Omnicom owns an advertising agency which is losing revenue as a client shifts away from broadcast advertising to promotions, it can hedge its position by investing in a good independent promotions firm servicing the same client and together the two firms should be able to refer work between each other and hence generate incremental revenue above what they would have obtained independently. In essence, they are leveraging the client relationship as far as possible.

On the people side, synergy may exist between services as disparate as auditing and strategy consulting work. In both cases, the core skills the firm has will be managing a client relationship, understanding the commercial challenges they face and bringing outstanding talent to bear on the problem. All PSFs share a common challenge—how to attract and retain outstanding people. The better the people a firm can put against a client task, the better will be the client relationship.

A firm that is excellent at managing its professionals should be able to leverage exactly the same skill in any firm it acquires. The managerial expertise required for PSFs is pretty much universal to the industry. Therefore, a PSF that has mastered this expertise in one firm should be able to extend itself fairly successfully into others.

VERTICAL INTEGRATION

Nor have PSFs been punished by the markets for their predilection for vertical integration. Many of the great integrated industrials of the 1960s have just about been broken up. The car manufacturers tend increasingly to use independent components suppliers, the paper mills are divesting their forests. All the emphasis is on focusing on core competencies combined with aggressive outsourcing. There is no credibility in insisting on extracting margin points from a wholly owned supply chain. Yet, despite this dominant mantra, the PSF sector tends to have moved progressively in the opposite direction. Firms offering advice to clients on their corporate design tend also to have Mac production departments, advertising agencies tend to have film producers in-house even if production itself is outsourced, investment banks have corporate financiers who foment the deals and salespersons who distribute the commercial paper to finance them.

In general, there has been a thrust by most PSFs to move upstream into advisory work and thereby control the flow of executional work to their engine rooms of production. The usual misperception is that PSFs are all battling upstream because this is where margins are better. While this can be the case, it is not the end of the story. Establishing a good upstream advisory position with major client organizations means that the PSF will have a strong hold on key senior relationships. This will position it well to influence the distribution of large volumes of implementation work which can usually be done by much more junior and cheaper people. Here the margins are typically very high, as we will come onto. That is why PSFs are often right to throw a number of highly paid people at high-level client contacts which can never yield a decent margin in their own right—if the executional work is then referred through, the investment will pay off. The investment banks, for example, may make relatively low returns directly off their investment in serried ranks of analysts but if these people then give a mandate to place a major equity issue, the bank will yield a high return in their sales and broking arm.

There are firms such as McKinsey or Boston Consulting Group who basically focus only on the high-end advisory work, avoid implementation and achieve very high margins. They do so because they have the credibility to sustain very high charge-out rates. This is not, however, a dominant strategy. Most PSFs operate on the economic principle of leverage and vertical integration, as we will explore presently.

The dominant strategy of the larger PSFs has been for global integration across a diverse set of disciplines rather than global extension along a single product line. As we have discussed, there are a number of reasons that global "bundling" has been the favoured approach—most significantly the opportunity of fostering cross-referral, exploiting operating "synergies" and hedging the nature of client demand (by, for example, owning both head-hunting firms and remuneration management firms to reduce the impact of the cyclical shift from one focus to the other on overall earnings). More often, however, it is simply the fastest and easiest way to expand quickly, particularly through acquisition. In effect, a bundling strategy can amount to portfolio management.

The problem with the portfolio approach in the professional service environment is that the key rain makers usually view their own discipline as the most important and the best people tend not to cluster in environments where they are part of a corporate trade-off. The result is that PSF segments which have been consolidated as part of portfolios are prone to suffer a gradual erosion of value added and margin decline. Hence there is a perennial problem of the mature firms in the portfolio creating independent spinoffs, and of disruptive schisms erupting between the more powerful members of the tribes. The Arthur Andersen/Andersen Consulting split is a classic example. The large, portfolio-holding companies are continually under pressure to specialize, although they haven't been constrained in the same way as their industrial counterparts such as ITT or Hanson, because of the more compelling synergies of common clients, interchangeable people and the similar management skills they require and which can be leveraged across a portfolio of PSFs.

GLOBAL VERSUS LOCAL SPECIALIZATION

The rival dominant strategy to global bundling is global product line specialization. In essence this amounts to sticking to the knitting and growing geographically rather than through product extensions and add-ons. It is essentially purist and reflects the logic of the core competence debate. McKinsey, for example, has resolutely remained focused on high-end corporate strategy consulting and has not meandered off into the alluring area of IT implementation and BPR. Sema Consulting has focused almost uniquely on IT-facilitated change issues. Such firms tend to be single-brand. Their culture will be fairly uniform globally and they will share resource and techniques actively. They tend to have been grown largely organically unlike their integrated counterparts who will have typically been very acquisitive. As a result they tend to have been around for a long time. It takes at least five years to get a new office up and running in most markets, marginally longer than it takes to successfully absorb a new acquisition!

There are, of course, a large number of outstanding specialists who have remained either national or regional. Lazard Freres and Flemings in corporate finance, Maritz in corporate incentives, and CAA in talent management are some better-known examples. This may be a viable form of defending a profitable niche, but in the end it is vulnerable to the global specialists as well as global integrated networks as clients globalize. Of course, such firms usually prove fairly hard to displace from the local market, like ancient limpets on rocks of steadfast client relationships—it took all the muscle of the US investment banking industry to dislodge the UK merchant banks and even now firms such as Flemings and Schroders are pre-eminent independent local players. However, they are susceptible to the ongoing acquisitiveness of larger specialized or bundled networks.

Nowadays, it is typically very hard for a local specialist to break into becoming a regional or global player. In most PSF segments it is now too late, with the exception of high-growth niches such as Internet advisory services. Also, they suddenly confront a new set of investment requirements they are not equipped to finance. Setting up two new offices abroad might require a couple of million dollars of negative cash flow apiece. Without access to equity markets and without the debt-carrying capacity, this can impose a crippling burden across a region. It is quite common to see smaller PSFs attempting to replicate the bundling strategies of global networks in their attempts to break this cycle. They might gain a stock market listing through a reverse takeover[2] and buy a few other PSFs locally in an endeavour to build scale and attract investor attention. Usually, however, they go nowhere. The graveyard of PSFs is in this intermediate territory. The dominant balance is a few large, integrated players, a lot of smaller specialists and a few underperforming, sometimes listed companies in the middle.

SECTOR VERSUS PRODUCT SPECIALIZATION

PSFs who chose to focus rather than integrate or bundle face a choice—either to extend on the basis of a product applicable across many client sectors or to grow on the basis of client sector knowledge. The product-led strategy is an inward-focused orientation. To succeed, the firm has to be more expert in its particular methodologies and approaches to problem solution than a generalist competitor. This has been the classic method of expansion for the PSF, through from the advertising agencies to the law firms. Stick to the knitting and, by virtue of developing a group of functionally specialized people, secure competitive advantage.

Sector specialization, by contrast, is a client-focused strategy. The PSF gains advantage by knowing more about the client's industry than the client does itself. Its underlying rationale is that the difference between the competitive dynamics of different industries is far more important to the client than expertise about how to deploy a general technique in the unique context of the client. Since the methodologies most functionally specialized PSFs deploy are hardly rocket-science and can be readily copied, there is not much of a defensible advantage in terms of tools—anyone can conduct legal due diligence or distribute a small bond issue. However, thorough knowledge about a client sector, based on a working relationship with the key players, is highly defensible because such a PSF will tie up the critical relationships which unlock the knowledge of the sector.

Sector specialization is a far more recent phenomenon than product-led strategies. PSFs pursuing this line tend to have emerged as spin-offs from more generalist, integrated firms.

[2] In this context, a reverse takeover usually involves a private, unlisted company 'reversing' into a quoted company in order to obtain a listing for the enlarged group.

Although it is in its early stages, it is also proving extremely compelling with clients, for the simple reason that such firms will know much more about the peculiar competitive situation the client faces than a generalist firm. In a pitch situation there is usually no comparison. It is testimony to the power of sector specialization that many mature PSFs have moved to a multi-sector team structure. The investment banks, for example, will tend to have telecomms teams split out from consumer goods teams. The major consulting firms are slowly building reputations for sector expertise off the back of benchmarking products. While these client-led structures are typically matrixed with product-led departments, in most cases the client-led teams tend quickly to become the dominant force in the relationship.

EXECUTING A STRATEGY

It is hard to say whether specialized global product line or client sector expansion is a more or less successful strategy than bundling. The two strategies hold very different challenges. The global niche will tend to be built around expertise and give the PSF more cachet and negotiating power with both clients and potential employees. The global bundling strategy tends to be driven by objectives relating to capturing maximum client spend and can suffer the margin challenges of client exclusivity. It also suffers the risk of loss of focus and the challenge of coordination. Global specialist players tend by comparison to be highly coordinated and leverage resources globally with great effectiveness. It is usually easier for them to achieve outstanding margins as a result.

Whichever of the two dominant strategies a firm pursues, how a firm chooses to put together its network is another issue entirely. It usually has a choice of funding start-ups, all-out acquisition or a variety of investment arrangements from affiliations, joint ventures, investment relationships (which usually means below 20% participation and dividends from which are treated as "investment income" for accounting purposes) to "associates" of between 20% and 50% (which typically are consolidated at the operating profit level), to majority shareholdings which can be fully consolidated for financial purposes (less any minority interests).

Acquisitions

Since each PSF is a bundle of unique people, customs, culture and client relationships held together by a glue of loyalty, predatory acquisitions are not usually that successful. The exceptions are in the case of institutionalized brands where the impact of individual defections is mitigated (an obvious example being the highly successful takeover of J. Walter Thompson by WPP Group plc in 1987).

More common is a slow incrementalist creep. Typically this might begin with the forging of a non-equity association between the target and acquisitor. This allows the buyer to get an understanding of how the firm works, and also lowers the barriers as relationships form and clients are referred. It also gives them time to understand the firm's financials and shareholding structures better. This will typically be followed by minority stakes and then an option over a majority shareholding until assimilation is complete. In the case of a research firm, for example, a cold acquisition might cost ten times profits after tax whereas the extension of a minority share into a majority share of an associate might only cost five times. Of course, one route takes a few months and the other a few years.

In general, it is more common for global integrators or bundlers to acquire and for global specialist players to grow organically. This means that their respective growth trajectories are fundamentally different. J. Walter Thompson took 130 years and WPP 12 years to get where they are today. Since goodwill either does not have to be written off against earnings or only over a long period under GAAP rules (depending on the country),[3] integrators can grow earnings faster than global niche

---

[3] In the USA a majority buyer can consolidate an acquisition under "pooling of interest" which literally involves an amalgamation of the P&L and balance sheet. Under this scenario there is no goodwill to be amortized at all. In the case of a non-pooling event which creates goodwill, this can be written off over 40 years. Since most deals will not happen at a valuation of more than 15–20 times profits after tax, the rate of amortization is much slower than the boost to earnings for the acquirer. In the UK currently goodwill can be written off straight to reserves, so it has no P&L impact at all, therefore not dampening reported consolidated earnings. This rule is now changing and, in future, firms will either be able to capitalize it and revalue the goodwill annually (with any resulting charge hitting earnings) or amortize it over 20 years. In any of these cases, firms have full leeway to treat goodwill in a way which will not significantly affect their ability to consolidate any company they acquire with a net increase in earnings, thereby boosting their own EPS.

players and hence accelerate value generation for shareholders in terms of EPS. Since the average acquisition will have a cash payback of around seven years (assuming a multiple of ten times profits after tax), this does not in fact translate into free cash flow and on a cash basis it is likely the organic route to growth will yield higher free cash flow over that first initial period (although not necessarily in the longer term).

Joint venturing

Joint venturing is an increasingly common way for industrials to reap the benefits of merger without committing the capital to it or risking the managerial distraction. As a result it is not frowned upon by the markets in the same way as acquisition. Over the past ten years joint ventures have blossomed, often involving the formation of virtual entities to act as vehicles for the collaboration. These industrial alliances sometimes only exist to serve a temporary customer need and, once it is satisfied, they disband. In other cases they mature into formal mergers.

For the PSF industry, by contrast, joint ventures are anathema. It is rare to find two firms of a similar size joint venturing in any situation other than where a common client has forced a more cooperative approach between its suppliers. It is fairly common for multinational PSFs to take minority positions in smaller firms in countries where they have no presence. But such arrangements are almost always viewed by the larger firm as a prelude to acquisition (it is cheaper to buy firms you know and where you have some leverage!).

The usual reason driving PSFs away from cooperation is that their assets can easily walk between firms and their "technologies" are readily transferable. The mindset is one of guarded insecurity. There is nothing institutionally to encourage cooperation, particularly as most individual incentives relate to personal financial performance. If a larger PSF encounters another PSF regularly in the course of its activity on a large client, it will almost certainly consider buying it, not joint venturing with it.

Organic growth

Given cooperation is a no-go and acquisitions are expensive, the big problem most PSFs face is how to sustain high levels of organic growth. On a cash basis, organic growth offers a surer short-term cash return than acquisition because incremental revenue drops cash to the bottom line faster. If a team is hired, it will usually only take a year before they are achieving the firm's average rate of return. Payback may, therefore, be between one and two years. By contrast, most PSF acquisitions will occur at around ten times after tax earnings, so that cash payback will be between five and seven years assuming the firm can grow the target faster than it was growing alone. On an accounting basis, however, the goodwill associated with an acquisition often either does not have to be amortized against earnings or only over a long period (depending on the territory) while the earnings of the target can be fully consolidated. On an accounting basis acquisitions therefore usually offer far quicker rewards than organic growth, boosting reported earnings and EPS much more swiftly. This in part has fuelled the rate of acquisition among quoted PSFs.

The organic growth challenge has its toughest hurdle in the project-based nature of work. Since clients tend to employ PSFs to fulfil discrete tasks such as a PR campaign, a new stock issuance or legal due diligence, it becomes pretty hard for most PSFs to plan for growth with the certainty of industrials. As we will come onto, growth is limited by billing capacity and it is therefore impossible to grow without investing in new people. Since most PSFs are not properly capitalized, the decision to invest is a major one. Often firms won't do it without reasonably certain client commitment to new work, which throws the firm into the classic chicken and egg situation. As a result, they will often creep forward in fits and starts. More commonly they will stall at around $3million in fee income, locked into a cycle of project work—each piece of work will have to be repitched, and each client rewon. The demanding process of keeping the existing ball in the air will tend to distract energy (and often quite rightly as we will discuss) away from winning entirely new clients. The focus will be uniquely on farming without growth. The longer this pattern persists the more likely it is that the firm will stagnate rather than burst the magic bubble of the $3 million mark. At heart, it is a balance sheet issue.

The project paralysis syndrome can be broken by shifting gear from hand to mouth to long term, relationship based work. The key is usually to crack and penetrate two or three major clients so that the firm becomes the undisputed favoured supplier. This might even be enshrined in an annual contract but is more likely to take the form of a small monthly retainer coupled with un-pitched annual projects. Once a stable set of cash flows are established the firm will be in a position to begin to invest in the professional talent necessary to pitch successfully for new work. Interestingly, once this virtuous cycle is set in motion, of a significant percentage of billings coming from a handful of mature repeat relationships, then the firm will tend to grow without this pattern altering (provided, of course, that it remains competitive). In a successful, high-growth PSF, the golden ratio of stable repeat client work to revenue will tend to hover around 50%. The negative side is that it can translate in time into undue client dependency as we will come onto. But in practical terms it is the only way a PSF can break into the medium-size league unless it has a well-funded balance sheet, which is rarely the case.

Pulling it all together

So how do firms add value through either a strategy of specialization or integration bundling? Both dominant strategies lay claim to cost advantages, notably in the back-office area. Large groups, particularly those operating internationally, are usually able to depress their effective tax charge by applying tax credits generated by losses in one operation to earnings elsewhere and also by consolidating through offshore vehicles where tax rates are advantageous. They are also able to reap scale economies in treasury, lowering borrowing costs (including using excess cash to fund working capital without incurring real interest charges) and amortizing capital costs over a larger revenue base. Finally, they can exploit scale economies in areas such as purchasing, IT and financial control. In a group sized, say, around $1 billion this might add up to between one and three margin points to the bottom line versus each operating company doing such activities alone on a like-for-like basis. However, that is a static benefit ratio. The only question is, will the firms perform as well as part of a global integrator as they would alone?

In terms of revenue generation advantages, the two dominant strategies are quite distinct. First, as already discussed, the bundler or integrator might be able to smooth the earnings cycle of the group by managing the holding as a portfolio. The communications group with 50% of revenues in promotions and 50% in advertising might be able to ride the cycle of client spend more efficiently than either would be able to do alone. If it holds a blend of small firms and large it might also be able to mitigate the higher volatility and risk associated with smaller PSFs with the stable cash flows of its bigger firms. This would mean that although all its assets did not have the quality of earnings of a large network, a holding might be able to maintain a credit rating undiluted by the higher volatility of the smaller members, hence lowering borrowing costs and increasing shareholder value.

Both integrators and global specialists boast the benefits of cross-referral—that is, revenue which is incremental to the sum of the revenues of the companies as stand-alone entities. In a larger bundled holding with a diverse group of firms with common clients the maximum referral number can be considerable, say up to 10% of revenue. But again referral in a global specialist player will be intrinsically more efficient between geographies than it is likely to be between different product lines in a bundled player. Firms such as Boston Consulting Group efficiently pass clients and sector knowledge from office to office. It would not be uncommon for a client sourced on the West Coast of the USA to be serviced in London a year later.

The issue is, do any of the value-adding mechanisms of cross-referral and cost synergies outweigh the natural growth momentum that derives from specialist knowledge? Medium-sized PSFs within the structure of an integrated holding tend not to grow faster than their specialized and independent counterparts. There are many anomalies to this pattern such as the large consulting arms of the accountancy firms. However, the consultancy partners in such situations are typically specialists who will fight for the integrity of their products and client relationships. There is no overpowering evidence that integration in PSFs is more advantageous than global specialization. The most successful bundled firms are, in fact, collections of global specialists with their own operating integrity and brands.

In summary, the two key strategic battle terms in PSFs are synergy versus specialization. Synergy basically means leveraging individual client relationships. Specialization means refining targeted skills and monopolizing targeted professionals. One strategy is focused internally and the other externally. In the battle between synergy and specialization, specialization is likely to be the winner over the next decade. Clients are continuing to show a dominant propensity to unbundle. As PSFs mature it is likely that they will follow, although at the moment the strategic momentum from the supply side is actually towards integration. A few good firms will run the gamut and manage a matrix of the two—groups of specialists running under distinct brands but capitalizing on the benefits of cross-referral. Firms such as IPG, Omnicom and WPP, within the marketing services world, are flourishing on such matrixed arrangements. But most PSFs will be forced to choose their strategy. Bundling cannot be justified on the basis of back-office integration alone. There has to be a compelling revenue advantage.

The issue facing firms that have opted for specialization will be whether to specialize by product or by client sector. This tension between product-and-client based organization is already emerging in many PSFs. Firms such as McKinsey and many of the investment banks have a certain level of sector-based resource, with their client sector teams in areas such as telecomms and consumer goods. But these still tend to be pinned onto traditional product area structures such as M&A, corporate finance, stock analysis, etc. Empirically, it seems that sector- or client-oriented structures lead to greater competitiveness than more traditional forms of organization. But the bets are still out. Again, the best firms will tend to be experts at matrix management.

5
How Do You Tell How a PSF is Doing?

The standard financial variables used to measure industrial performance such as return on equity, asset turns and balance sheet leverage are not that helpful with PSFs. They are oriented to firms whose primary asset is capital and an order book. The primary asset of the PSF is the assets that don't register on the balance sheet—people and the goodwill of client relationships. They therefore qualify for special treatment.

The key to all businesses is free cash flow; that is, cash available for distribution to shareholders after all necessary capital expenditure and minority interests. What matters as far as shareholders are concerned is how efficiently the firm converts revenue into free cash flow and how much free cash flow it generates relative to the equity invested in it—in other words, cash return on equity. PSFs are usually very efficient generators of cash flow, converting large amounts of revenue into free cash which can be returned to shareholders. Since little capital is required, cash return on equity is usually very high indeed.

The measure that matters for PSFs is profit generated per shareholder or partner which is the equivalent of EPS[1] in an industrial firm. In a PSF structured as a partnership the partner's time represents their equity. They are therefore focused on maximizing income per partner. In a PSF structured as a normal limited company with shareholders, the senior managers are

---

[1] EPS = earnings per share

focused on maximizing profit per share or return on equity. While the two measures (profit per partner and per share) are somewhat different in appearance, they basically measure the same thing.

So what drives a PSF's ability to maximize income per partner or per share? The first thing that matters is the firm's ability to generate fees. Its profit capacity will be determined by its 'fee capacity'. Fee capacity is simply the product of the number of professionals at different levels of the organization who undertake client work, the utilization of these people on client work and their average hourly charge-out rate (Figure 5.1). Fee capacity is the theoretical maximum income the firm is able to generate given its professional base.

Fee capacity is all very well but it means nothing if it is not converted into profit. The conversion of fee capacity into profit is a multi-stage process (Figure 5.2). The first issue that keeps good managers awake at night is the "realization" of fee capacity— that is, what percentage of fee capacity is actually turned into revenue. It is a measure of whether the professionals in a firm are as utilized as they should be and whether it is charging the prices it should be (assuming it has the correct professional structure). The second issue is the efficiency with which it turns revenue per professional into contribution per professional. Contribution is calculated as revenues less direct costs, principally the cost of

Level of organization	# professionals	Total hours available *	Utilization or 'billability'	Hourly rate £	Fee capacity £ (000)
'Partner'	7	13 440	25%	200	672
2	10	19 200	40%	140	1075
3	15	28 800	80%	100	2304
4	40	76 800	90%	75	5184
'Graduate recruit'	100	192 000	100%	45	8640
Total	172	330 240	——	——	17 875

* Assumes 240 days a year and 8 hours a day

Figure 5.1 *Illustrative calculation of fee capacity for a PSF*

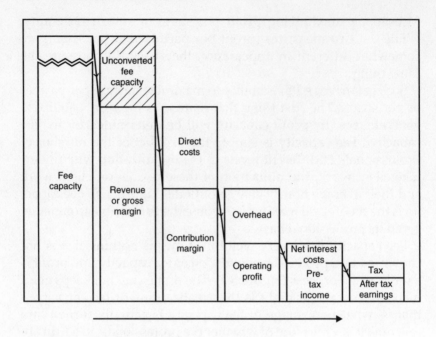

Figure 5.2   *Simplified stages of conversion of fee capacity into profit in a PSF*

employees. Contribution is a measure of a firm's ability to control direct costs, the biggest cost item on the P&L.

The third issue which keeps good managers awake is the firm's ability to turn contribution into distributable income or the operating margin on revenue of the firm. This is principally a measure of the firm's ability to control non-staff overhead costs such as property, expenses and support functions. Finally, there is the pre-tax margin. The principal item between the operating margin and the pre-tax margin is interest income and expense. The ability to control the interest line is a direct reflection of the efficiency of the management of the balance sheet, as we will come onto in Chapter 7. These four conversion processes will dictate the firm's ability to generate profit per partner or per share. Since there is very little difference in PSFs between reported after-tax profits (after deduction of any payments due to minority interests) and free cash flow, it is also a driver of the firm's ability to generate free cash flow (Figure 5.3).

Level of organization	Fee capacity £ (000) ①	Direct costs	Contribution	Overhead allocation *	Operating profit	Operating profit per partner
Partner	672	440	232	440	–208	–28
2	1075	600	475	600	–125	–18
3	2304	1000	1304	1000	304	43
4	5184	2100	3084	2100	984	141
Graduate recruit	8640	3400	5240	3400	1840	263
Total	17 875	7540	10 335	7540	2795	401

* Allocated based on direct costs

① See figure 5.1

Figure 5.3 *Illustrative calculation of potential profit per partner (000s)*

Few firms bother to think about their business in terms of these drivers of profits per share and per partner. Instead they focus on a simpler set of measures. The standard measures of performance divide into top-line and bottom-line ratios relating to the two discrete areas all PSFs have to worry about—growing client revenues and controlling the cost of delivery. These two sets of variables are obviously related but can move independently. On the revenue side the key metric is:

• Revenues per professional and growth in revenues per professional

and on the cost side, there is the inverse of the same coin:

• The ratio of staff costs-to-revenue

These two metrics reflect the simple cost structure of most professional service firms. The key to PSF profitability is the ability to win client revenues and to convert revenue into margin by managing staff costs and productivity. This relationship between the top and bottom line is referred to as the firm's "conversion rate". A PSF's conversion rate is a measure of its incremental profit divided by its incremental revenue (e.g. 1997 revenue and profit minus 1996 revenue and profit). The better a firm is able to convert a high percentage of incremental revenue into profit, the more efficiently it will create wealth for shareholders.

THE BALANCE SHEET

The balance sheet of most PSFs is incredibly simple, reflecting the fact that most of the assets are intangible. Most PSFs tend to have very little leverage or long-term obligations, funding themselves mostly through managing working capital and retained earnings. Since most PSFs have fairly low capital investment requirements, they dividend out most of their earnings after tax available for distribution and consequently the balance sheets tend to have low net asset values. Since there is little depreciation and capex, the overall balance sheet will tend to be small in total relative to the revenues of the business.

As a result, the key for most PSFs is their ability to manage their working capital effectively and hence their cash flow. The only real issue with most PSF balance sheets is the net working capital position. The good signs are an ability to generate prepaid expenses or retainers and their associated phenomenon, decent interest earnings. The concerning signs are large accumulations of work in progress (WIP), the PSF equivalent to inventory, and a history of write-offs or provisions for write-offs. Obviously, a negative net current assets position over the course of the year would cause concern since it would indicate likely future working capital problems.

There is also the issue of seasonality. Since most PSFs are very lightly capitalized, large gaps between work in progress accumulated and receipt of payment can create havoc in financial solvency, creating a need for deep overdraft facilities. Even though a debt position may have evaporated by year-end, it will leave behind the dirty stain of high interest expenses on the P&L. Most PSFs have low undividended cash reserves, so good working capital management is the difference between life and death. We will come onto how PSFs can optimize this presently.

The other key to note with PSFs are off-balance sheet and unfunded or contingent liabilities. The biggest is usually the building. Since it is usually the only true fixed cost in the business, it is the thing which ultimately sets the point of "break-even"[2] for any PSF. It is often a big temptation for firms to move into expensive premises. The key assets are people and clients, and good office space has a tangible influence on the ability of a firm to attract both. The question is, how exposed does this leave the firm to downturns? The current cost per square foot of the building is not the only concern; most buildings are leased and different leases will bind the firm into future obligations such as rate reviews and non-sublet clauses. The issue therefore extends beyond current cost to the length of the lease, the cost of lease breaks, the frequency of rent reviews, and clauses governing subletting. If any of these are onerous, the economics of any PSF can switch violently from boom to bust. The building is the apocryphal PSF killer.

Another major item can be capital leases of items such as computers, servers, photocopiers and production equipment. Again, the same applies to them as it does to building leases. If the number is mounting relative to revenues the firm is simply increasing the risk attached to its cash flows. In general, however, the balance sheet is not where the action is with PSFs. The action all happens on the P&L.

THE P&L

The first thing on the P&L is revenues. This wouldn't seem too complex. However, classifying revenues is probably the toughest part with PSF accounting. Many PSFs have a high volume of "pass-through costs"—that is, costs which are in fact just bought-in services provided by a third party and which the client could buy-in separately but allows the PSF to manage in return for a mark-up. Pass-through costs will typically carry a very low mark-up margin because clients quickly catch on that they are paying unnecessary commission. However, they can be used to inflate the revenue line significantly when revenue is not really being earned by the firm. Rather than revenue, this aggregate number is better referred to as turnover or "billings" and does not accurately reflect the economic size of the firm. As

---

[2] Break-even is measured as revenues minus direct costs divided by fixed costs. As soon as this ratio equals one or more, the firm will have generated enough contribution to cover its overhead or, in other words, it will have broken even.

a result, most PSFs are better looked at on a "gross margin" basis.

The gross margin of a PSF is the revenue yielded from charges for work actually performed by the firm, and excludes the cost of bought-in services. As such, it represents genuine revenue. The problem with this distinction between billings and gross margin is that firms can account for them differently and there is often a lack of clarity surrounding what costs have been included and what is not included in the gross margin number.

This means that calculating comparable operating profit margins between PSFs is not straightforward. Operating margins based on billings are clearly not meaningful since the margins a firm achieves on pass-through costs will typically be much lower than those it can achieve on work it actually performs. Much more meaningful are margins on gross income or revenue which reflect the efficiency with which it can charge for and perform the work itself. Using gross margins for purposes of financial assessment means making sure that all direct staff costs associated with the firm are applied after the calculation of gross margin and not before (Figure 5.4).

It is also worth noting that many small, privately held PSFs tend to inflate their operating margins because of their treatment of aspects of salary costs. First, most reward key employees based on bonuses which can easily exceed base pay. Bonuses are often calculated as a percentage of the profits before tax, even though they are really an operating cost item. They therefore sometimes get excluded in the basic pre-tax operating profit numbers, thus significantly inflating the apparent operating margin.

Second, the equity owners of many smaller PSFs will tend to take the bulk of their interests in dividends from distributable profits rather than as pre-tax bonuses. This is often less tax efficient (depending on the country) but is often the way they choose to do it. The result is that the operating margin numbers are again inflated as they do not reflect the full effective salary expectations of the partners. In any acquisition situation the numbers tend to have to be adjusted down to reflect the inclusion of market rates of salary for partners.

As we have already discussed, people costs are the biggest slice of the cost pie (Figure 6.5) for all PSFs and therefore the staff cost to revenue ratio is a critical guide to performance. Typically,

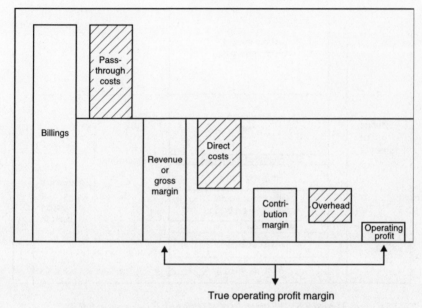

Figure 5.4 *Calculating real margins in a PSF using Billings*

a staff–revenue ratio in excess of 60% suggests that the firm is not managing its direct costs effectively and is probably suffering from a combination of overstaffing and overpay. As a general rule a competitive PSF will want to aim to charge clients at least twice the fully loaded cost of their people;[3] in the consulting industry this multiple will typically average out at around three and a half times. This would imply a staff–revenue ratio somewhere under 40%.

The non-staff costs of PSFs are usually bundled together in a nebulous pile called "other costs", often adding up to as much as 30–35% of revenue or gross margin. The problem with this pile is that it is often hard to understand exactly what it is and therefore whether overhead items are being well or poorly managed. One of the constituents will usually be out-of-pocket expenses which were not billed to the client, such as travel and entertainment. Failure to bill expenses is a classic sign of cost-control problems and probably poor working relationships with the client base that might feed through into disadvantageous pricing.

---

[3] Fully loaded employee costs will include pension contributions, car allowance, medical and other benefits, including bonus provisions.

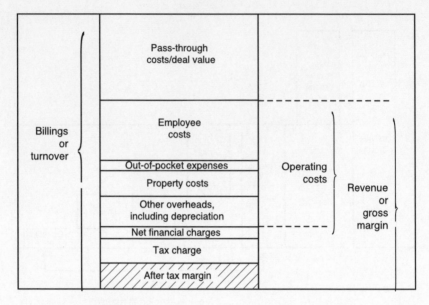

Figure 5.5   *Illustrative cost structure for a generic PSF*

The largest constituent of the overhead pile will be the lease and ancillary costs of the building. If this number alone is in excess of 12–15% of revenue it is likely that the firm has fallen into the trap of over-renting, always an ominous sign. A third item is likely to be a depreciation charge for capital items such as computers and office equipment. This is usually of less concern since it is periodic and necessary. The rest, perhaps amounting to a third of the total overhead pile, will relate to the back-office functions of the firm—a curious miscellany of costs, ranging from accountancy and audit to car leasing. As long as it is containable within 10% of revenue it is unlikely to be a problem. As we have already discussed, one of the keys to financial performance in any PSF is the ease with which it can break even. An excessive overhead burden will force the firm to increase its contribution margin[4] and drag down the ability of the firm to sustain a competitive rate of pay and hence damage its revenue-generating ability. Overhead is quite simply death for PSFs.

One key item which is often excluded from the overhead pile is

---

[4] Contribution margin is calculated as revenues minus direct costs, as a percentage of revenues. It represents the margin available to cover overhead.

the cost of non-professional staff—a wide range of people, from secretaries to accountants who are not directly client billable. They are, however, often included in the staff cost pile on the P&L. The effect is to distort the true overhead situation of the firm. The difference between one secretary per senior professional and one for every five professionals clearly makes a major difference to the cost structure. The problem with including them in direct staff costs is that these indirect staff costs will not be properly managed. Utilization or "billability"[5] will always appear lower than it actually is and lead to poor pricing and staffing decisions. Overhead will also look correspondingly lower than it actually is, again leading to poor decisions about adding further overhead costs.

The difference between the operating margin and the pre-tax margin is the balance of interest expense and income (although it may also include exceptional and other income and expenses, including investment income from minority positions in other companies). Heavy interest expense bodes poorly for PSFs since fixed-interest obligations have the same effect as overhead—they tend to force the PSF to focus on lowering costs rather than adding them to grow the revenue line. Interest income, by contrast, usually implies good management of working capital which is the key to survival of PSFs as they tend to be under-capitalized. In most PSFs there is little difference between operating margins and pre-tax margins because the net interest line is awash. Instead, it is the after-tax line that matters more since it represents the earnings distributable to shareholders.

After-tax profits are particularly revealing with a PSF because they do not differ substantially from free cash flow. Capex is typically no more than 5% of revenue, depreciation is correspondingly small and most more mature PSFs maintain a zero net fixed capital increase, whereby capex and depreciation offset each other. Most PSFs also strive to ensure that they do not have a deteriorating net working capital position year on year by achieving a rapid billing cycle with key clients. Hence there is

[5] Billability is another word for utilization commonly used in PSFs —that is, the percentage of professional time that is billed to the client. Some firms choose to use utilization to describe the level of activity of their professionals on client work irrespective of whether this time can be charged. In such a case, utilization will differ from billability since not all the work will be billable. Failure to focus on true billability or revenue generating utilization is a common pitfall amongst PSFs.

usually little change in net working capital. It would not be unusual for free cash flow to be greater than 80% of after-tax profits for a well-run PSF (without minority interests). So in PSFs it is a fair statement to say that profit is king (as opposed to the cliché about cash flow!).

The effective tax rate of PSFs tends not to be as volatile year on year as that of industrials since they have fewer items they can write off against tax and tend not to have loss carryforwards since few PSFs can survive repeated losses. Also few PSFs have sophisticated tax-planning strategies. Therefore, the effective tax rate in PSFs tends to be close to the statutory tax rate which, once again, makes the operating profits number the key number a firm has to focus on for management purposes.

THE P&L, TIMING AND GROWTH

As with industrials, the P&L of PSFs is not a static account. There is a significant issue surrounding the timing of revenue, costs and hence margin. The ability to shift revenue and also costs between periods can make a great difference to the apparent performance year on year. This might take the form of accruals or simply the crediting and debiting of cost and revenue for periods where there is some discretion for the accounting event. The usual reason for manipulating timing is to smooth the apparent earnings movements year on year. In a comparatively "dynamic" revenue environment, there is a great premium among PSFs to smoothing out earnings since it gives investors a sense of comfort they often feel they lack with PSFs. For anyone trying to understand underlying performance it, of course, creates problems.

In most PSFs revenue growth is no substitute for profitability. Whereas industrial or service firms can experience high growth while in a loss-making position and retain value because, in time, scale will allow break-even to be exceeded, most PSFs don't have scale economies. Break-even tends to occur at quite a low level and incremental revenue tends only to feed through to an increasing margin at a gentle incremental conversion rate (say, 1% margin improvement for every 10% of revenue growth). The reason is that direct resource tends to have to be added in line

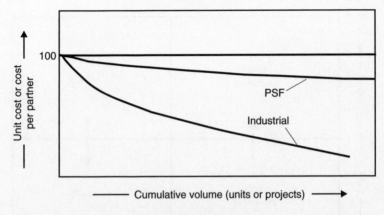

Figure 5.6 *Illustrative behaviour of unit costs in a typical PSF versus an industrial firm*

with added revenue and, since there are few fixed costs, costs in general therefore rise in line with growth (Figure 5.6). This means that an unprofitable, high-growth PSF should not be viewed as simply the rising star it might be were it an industrial. Margin is the key yardstick.

IT'S NOT JUST THE FINANCIALS . . .

The problem with the financials of PSFs, as with any talent-based firm, is that they do not tell the full story. What really drives those numbers is the ability of the firm to attract and retain both outstanding clients and outstanding professionals. Unless there is a balance between outputs and inputs the financial perform- ance of the firm will decline. In the PSF industry there is no such concept as the "cash cow"[6] whereby a business can be milked for years without reinvestment in order to maximize cash flow.

The best measure of outputs is client acquisition and churn. The highly competitive PSF will typically have a very low degree of client churn as it becomes an indispensable part of the client's value chain. J. Walter Thompson, for example, has serviced some

---

[6] The cash cow is a concept coined by Boston Consulting Group. It means a firm or business which can be sustained with low levels of investment in order to maximize the amount of free cash it throws off.

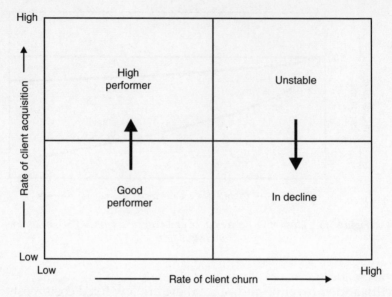

Figure 5.7 *Illustrative relationship between client churn and client acquisition
in a PSF*

major clients such as Unilever and Ford for over half a century.
Even in professional service segments which are characterized
by project work rather than continuous assignments, the longevity of relationships is a vital driver of profitability. Investment
banks, for example, may only receive a commission every three
years for a piece of M&A from a particular client but the profit
from a string of assignments over twenty years can be very high,
particularly as the costs of client acquisition and familiarization
will be negligible.

The counterpart of churn is client acquisition. The relationship
between churn and acquisition is illustrated in Figure 5.7. In
general, a firm with low churn and low acquisition will fare
better than a firm with high churn and high acquisition, because
it will incur lower unamortizable client-acquisition costs.[7] Client
acquisition, like M&A, is seen as exciting and sexy but can often
distract a firm from nurturing its core business. However, the
inverse also holds true to some extent. Unless a firm maintains a
decent trickle of new projects it will prove tough for it to attract

---

[7] Although client acquisition costs are in effect an investment, they have to be charged
straight to the P&L and not capitalized.

the quality of people necessary to feed its core accounts; boredom will set in, the firm may get the reputation for being lacklustre and major clients may begin to slip. Churn will then accelerate. There is therefore a delicate dynamic between churn and acquisition in good-performing PSFs.

In terms of the second key dimension of performance, inputs, the ability of a firm to attract and maintain talent will be a primary driver of its ability to grow profits. Again the core indicator is churn. If a firm is not able to retain and grow its professionals then its profit potential will be sharply eroded as it fails to cultivate business farmers[8] and then turn them into business winners. It will suffer the high costs associated with a heavy hiring cycle. It will also lose its individual knowledge base to competitors and hence its ability to differentiate itself.

Conversely, all firms need to maintain a throughput of new professionals. A firm that is an efficient hirer will typically only need to hire at junior graduate level and then promote and fire from its core employee group to feed senior ranks. Accordingly, the market presence of a PSF will be fairly accurately reflected in the degree of awareness of the firm on graduate campuses. McKinsey, for example, will typically be the highest aspiration for most business school graduates. This will be directly reflected in the applications per advertised slot and also in their market share of graduates from the top MBA schools such as Harvard, Stanford, Wharton and INSEAD. A competitive advertising agency, for example, can expect to receive in excess of a thousand applications for every job posting.

Employee and client churn can be viewed as the two sides of the long-term slice of the balance sheet of a PSF, with the clients on the asset side and the professionals on the liabilities side. If a firm achieves equilibrium in low client churn and low professional churn then it will almost certainly be highly competitive. If a firm underfunds its assets by depressing staff levels, then it will begin to erode its balance sheet, something that is certain to hit profits further down the road. If, on the other hand, it fails to keep its professional capital well employed then it will suffer poor margins. The current part of the PSF balance sheet is client

---

[8] "Farmers" is the term used to describe professionals focused on increasing billings from existing clients by winning new projects from them. The term is commonly used across all PSF sectors.

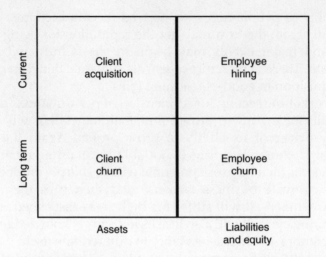

Figure 5.8   Drivers of the human balance sheet of the PSF

acquisition and professional hiring which obey the same dynamics as the long term part of the balance sheet. Of course, as we have discussed, the long term and current pieces of the balance sheet need to be in balance in turn (Figure 5.8).

In general, the human balance sheet of the PSF is actually more informative about a firm's future performance than its financial balance sheet!

6
Understanding the Underlying Economics of a PSF

Underlying the P&L and balance sheet of all PSFs are the real economic drivers of the firm. The key determinant of the profit per partner or per share is the fee capacity of the firm and the cost of providing that fee capacity. Fee capacity, as we have already discussed, is determined by:

Organizational structure
The number of professionals employed at different levels in the organization

×

Utilization
The percentage of their time they spend client billable

×

Charge-out rates
How much they charge a client for an hour of their time

ORGANIZATIONAL STRUCTURE

The structure of a firm will determine its capacity for growth. Four partners operating alone may be able to charge sufficiently to sustain a highly competitive margin. However, their capacity to grow the absolute revenues of the firm will be constrained. The answer is, of course, the pyramidal hierarchy which allows the partners to leverage their client relationships into much larger revenue bases and to leverage their own time across more client-acquisition activity. Leverage is simply the ratio of partners or business winners (often known as hunters or rain makers) to doers or staffers. This principle of leverage has driven the evolution of the PSF organizational structure. In some cases the firm's professional structure may look like a barrel with an even level of professionals at all levels. In others it may be an apple core with few middle-rankers. More commonly it is a pyramid with a differing size base relative to the size of the apex (Figure 6.1).

Two of the key benefits of leverage are the ability to yield profitable revenues from clients and the ability to gain new client assignments. In terms of farming, the partner usually has to maintain and develop the client relationship. To do so they usually have to play a hand in the overall strategy of the account. However, it will clearly be more profitable for cheaper professionals to actually get much of the work done. Introducing more soldiers to the account will allow the PSF to grow the volume of revenues from the particular client. It will also free up the partners' time to both win new projects from the same client and also to bring in completely new business. More importantly, it will systematically increase margins.

In general, the margin on professional hours will increase, the further you go down the pyramid, as we will explore presently. This means that the greater the leverage, the greater will be the level of profitability on the account *per se*. Once you throw in the value of new business brought in by partners whose hands are not tied by client servicing, the broader the base of the organizational pyramid, the greater will be the profit per client. This, of course, has its limits. Most PSFs are constrained from taking leverage to an extreme. Clients will tend to demand at least the partial presence of the partner and the partner will become ineffectual if stretched across too many accounts. This will usually dictate the absolute possible ratio of non-partners to partners in any business. Of course, the type of work performed for the client will also put constraints on partner dilution.

As we will come onto, it is always possible to calculate the

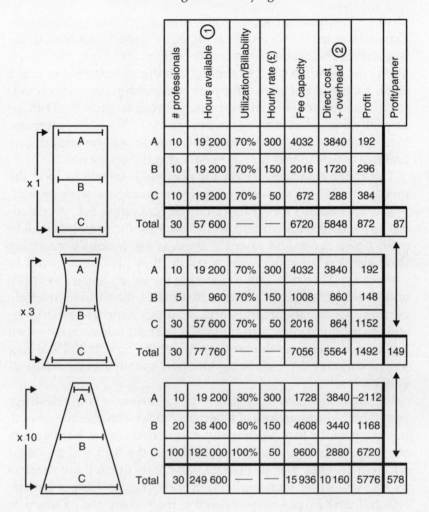

		# professionals	Hours available ①	Utilization/Billability	Hourly rate (£)	Fee capacity	Direct cost + overhead ②	Profit	Profit/partner
	A	10	19 200	70%	300	4032	3840	192	
x 1	B	10	19 200	70%	150	2016	1720	296	
	C	10	19 200	70%	50	672	288	384	
	Total	30	57 600	—	—	6720	5848	872	87
	A	10	19 200	70%	300	4032	3840	192	
x 3	B	5	960	70%	150	1008	860	148	
	C	30	57 600	70%	50	2016	864	1152	
	Total	30	77 760	—	—	7056	5564	1492	149
	A	10	19 200	30%	300	1728	3840	-2112	
x 10	B	20	38 400	80%	150	4608	3440	1168	
	C	100	192 000	100%	50	9600	2880	6720	
	Total	30	249 600	—	—	15 936	10 160	5776	578

① Assumes 240 days a year and 8 hours a day

② A = 200/hour, B = 90/hour, C = 15/hour fully loaded costs

Figure 6.1 *Illustrative calculation of partner leverage in a PSF*

ideal professional structure for a firm given client constraints. The main point is that few firms actually understand how structure drives their capacity to create billings and grow profitably. The usual reason for a PSF stalling is failure to extend beyond a small group of partners. The pure partnership can yield handsome incomes for each of the principals but its growth is fundamentally limited. It is also effectively unsaleable as an enterprise to another acquiror. Hence the classic family accountancy or law practice which sparks for a generation and then dies.

The other common reason for stalling is failure to feed the middle ranks of farmers and project managers with enough work. This results in the hierarchy degenerating into an eaten-out apple core. This usually occurs because the principals fail to push down work and hoard it themselves, jealously guarding their client relationships. As a result, they also tend to fail to promote and are reluctant to increase the salary levels of experienced graduates since the gut instinct is that this will erode partner income. In fact, this hollowed-out structure usually results in a high turnover of both clients and professionals which will bite directly into the profitability of the firm. In PSFs, trying to make money through being low cost usually has a disastrous effect.

Failure to delegate work down the hierarchy not only destroys profitability through loss of leverage, it also damages the growth prospects of the firm. As already mentioned, unless partners are freed up to chase and win new business, the firm will go unfed and wither. They may be heavily personally utilized but the firm overall will suffer underutilization and hence profits per partner will fall despite partners "working their asses off". Failure to delegate also eats into the time partners have for training the next tier of managers. Failure to train in PSFs is not the easily dispensable nice-to-have of industrials—it eats straight into the future competitiveness of the firm. If a firm fails to train, the partners will also not be able to effectively delegate with confidence—hence the self-reinforcing downward spiral of many PSFs.

Many PSFs let their clients dictate their own structures. If the most important clients have six levels of hierarchy, PSFs will tend to mirror this in their own firm. Of course, the economics of a PSF are very different from those of most clients. This makes pure replication an expensive decision. Many PSFs take the view that the value is created by keeping the client happy. In fact, failure to optimize profits by refining the professional structure damages the quality of people and work and hence client satisfaction. The smart firms are obsessed with refining their structure on an ongoing basis, independent of the professional structures of their clients.

UTILIZATION

Most PSFs are obsessed with utilization or billability (see pages 59 and 152 for an explanation of the distinction between utilization and billability). Since professionals are a sort of fixed asset with an ongoing cost, the focus is usually on keeping them uniformly fully utilized. While this would appear to be the way to maximize billing capacity, things are not in fact so simple.

The target-utilization mix of PSFs should differ up and down the professional hierarchy. The optimum utilization mix in fact usually looks something like Figure 6.2 rather than a uniform rate of utilization. The reason is pretty simple. In order to main-

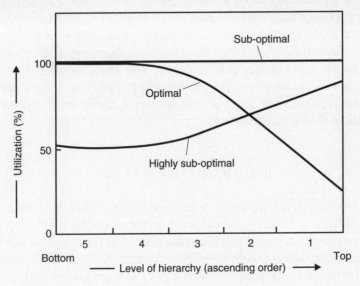

Figure 6.2   *Illustrative optimum utilization targets for a typical PSF*

tain forward momentum the partners of a PSF have to expend lots of time in non revenue-generating activity, such as developing client relationships, hiring good professionals and determining the direction of the firm. Unless the machine is fed it quickly dries up, particularly if a firm is driven by project-based work. Similarly, middle-ranking professionals have to spend a reasonable amount of time working on the farming process, otherwise long-term client relationships evaporate and profitability quickly withers. The result is that if utilization targets are set uniformly high across the entire firm then it may be temporarily profitable but business will quickly fall away.

The most junior ranks, the graduate recruits, have nothing to contribute other than billability. Therefore their target utilization can be much higher than that of partners. Indeed, unless their utilization is approaching 100% then it is a sure sign that the firm has too much capacity for its workload. The good firm will have utilization targets which are graded from 100% at the bottom to probably something around 30–40% at the top depending on the sector and the firm's positioning.

The failure to push through a differential utilization target will mean that the firm fails to optimize its structure and will underperform. Again, the usual reason this doesn't happen is the failure by management to push down work. Work hoarding is the psychological Achilles' heel of the PSF industry. Many executives assume that lowering utilization at the top will lower overall billing capacity and this belief pushes them towards uniform utilization. Of course, this is naive. The missing pieces of the puzzle are the average charge-out rate by level and the issue of business generation. As we will see, once these are factored in, the picture shifts dramatically.

CHARGE OUT RATES

The pricing structure of each level of the professional hierarchy will naturally differ. A senior partner, for example, might bill out at an hourly rate ten times that of a graduate recruit. This simple observation often leads managers to assume that more money can be made by deploying senior people than junior people. Of course, the internal ratio of senior to junior charge-out rates is not the relevant number. What matters is the charge out rate as a multiple of salary. Typically, this multiple increases down the hierarchy and with it the inherent profit margin per hour of professional time (Figure 6.3). It therefore makes more sense on a margin basis to use grunts where possible.

The charge-out rate at each level of professional is, of course, in part dictated by what the market will bear. While there is usually quite a lot of flexibility, it tends to fall into bands. The key about how a firm chooses to price within these generally accepted bands is that this will drive demand from clients for professional time. The charge-out rate directly drives the utilization structure of the firm. If, for example, grunts charge out at $30 an hour they will probably be fully utilized since clients will make use of that resource readily. A partner charging out at $500 an hour will probably only be utilized to a relatively low degree by clients requiring top-level input. Thus the pricing of resource drives the target utilization of a PSF through a natural market process.

The key trade-off in all PSFs therefore becomes the charge-out

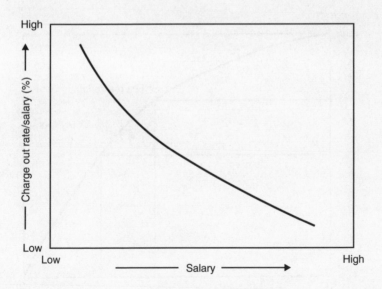

Figure 6.3 *illustrative relationship between charge-out rates and salary in a typical PSF*

rates against utilization which jointly drive the fee capacity potential of the business. In general, there is an optimal point for each PSF segment where the fee capacity will be maximized, taking into account the need for senior people in particular to have the non-billable time necessary to feed the business. This sweet spot is illustrated in the case of a consulting firm in Figure 6.4. Where this spot lies will vary from business to business depending on acceptable charge-out rates and the demands placed on senior professionals by their client base.

One typical mistake many PSFs make is to compress their charge-out rates; that is, to have a low multiple between the partner level and graduate recruit level. This usually means they are charging too little for their partner time and too much for their grunt time. The result is overutilization among partners where non-billable time is essential to grow the company and underutilization among grunts where there should be 100% utilization. The reason this happens is that the focus for all managers is typically on full utilization, often among partners included. As a result, senior people try to avoid overpricing themselves, particularly if they are being scrutinized by an

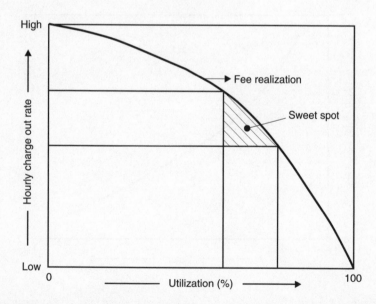

Figure 6.4   *illustrative maximization of fee or revenue realization in a PSF*

outside shareholder. As we have illustrated, this actually has the reverse effect from that intended—total company fee capacity will fall.

The other common mistake is not to maximize the multiple of salary that is effectively charged to the client by marginal increases in prices and by applying brakes on salary inflation. This means that cash is left on the table. The multiple of hourly fee price to cost is driven by the pricing strategy of the firm. We will come onto the issue of pricing strategies presently. But, in general, it is worth pointing out that many PSFs do not understand how to use price to influence profitability. All the emphasis is usually on utilization.

It is often assumed that clients are highly sophisticated when it comes to pricing and prevent flexibility in pricing strategies. In many PSF segments clients do have access to some sort of comparative pricing data across firms. However, when it comes to individual charge-out rates they tend to calibrate their sense of value against the quality of the people servicing their account. Therefore, the strict comparability of charge-out rates between firms lacks the clarity it usually has in most industrial settings. There are virtually no published price sheets and margin data is guarded closely by PSFs. This gives the PSF the discretion to make marginal shifts in hourly rates across the professional hierarchy without clients throwing their hands in the air. Marginal increases will flow straight to the bottom line.

On most PSF accounts clients will tend to look at the absolute sums of money charged for a project. As we will discuss presently, this is effectively a value-pricing mechanism rather than a strict hourly fee system. For the client it has the advantage of being easier to administer and budget for. This leaves it up to the discretion of the PSF to juggle its internal charge-out rates and utilization targets for the mix of professionals working on a particular job and fundamentally shift the profitability of the piece of work being done. The actual mathematics of the optimizing process are relatively simple as we have illustrated. But, despite this, it is unusual to find a PSF that plans systematically to maximize its fee capacity.

FEE CAPACITY AND RESOURCE ALLOCATION

As we have already explored, average utilization times the average charge-out rate times the number of professionals at each level determines the billing capacity of the company and the balance of these three elements also determines its margin potential. Each PSF, however, will tend to pursue a slightly different strategy on the fee-capacity matrix.

In terms of generic strategies, as we have discussed, the two dominant approaches are the specialist, focused partnership at one extreme and the large, integrated bundled network at the other. By picking the right structure both can achieve comparably high levels of income per partner. But, of course, they will focus on a quite distinct mix of the three drivers of fee capacity. The small specialist will have low leverage, uniformly high charge-out rates and high overall utilization. The partners themselves will tend to do the work. The integrated network, by comparison, will tend to have high leverage and a banded approach to utilization and charge-out rates. The partners will tend to be client figureheads and business feeders.

The firms which are suboptimal performers will tend to fall in the middle. They tend not to understand or even have thought about fee capacity. Charge-out rates will tend to reflect what is seen as the market norm, utilization targets will be woolly, and the professional structure unclear, with a proliferation of titles and ranks. Often they will bill clients based on a non-fees formula such as media commission or absolute project quotes. Over time this will have eroded their interest in logging hours, their ability to track professional utilization and their concern about cost structures. They may have no real sense of their equivalent charge-out rates and probably no sense of competitive charge-out rates. They will almost certainly not understand their staffing structure from an income-maximization standpoint and have little sense for how billable different professionals should be. The result will be suboptimal margins. Growth will also tend not to feed through to margin improvements. If the same error is repeated by many firms in a given PSF segment, this will tend to lead to a long-term depression of margins which will be unrecoverable as clients become accustomed to certain pricing and servicing norms.

Of course, fee capacity is only any good if it is matched by revenue or "realized". Fee capacity is also only any good if it is achieved with an appropriate mix of direct staff costs which allow the maximization of "contribution". The two-tier conversion of fee capacity into revenue and then contribution is the twin axis of PSF profitability. Decisive advantages are to be gained by all firms from calculating their optimal fee capacity and cost structure, by better understanding how much they can charge for their time, what utilization targets they should set and how they should structure their professional pyramid.

Having said that, in order to deliver the strategy, they also have to focus on the day-to-day allocation of professionals against tasks to ensure utilization and that each client project can support the target charge-out rates. It doesn't matter how robust the planning is, if the firm is not able to manage this process of allocation well the result will be mediocre.

Traditionally, most PSFs have managed the process of resource allocation by following their nose. Seasonal patterns become well known, as do the seasonal workloads of key clients. The problem with this approach is that there is no way of knowing whether the allocation has been optimized until the financial results come through when it is too late to adjust. Also, there tends to be a lot of corner cutting, such as lowering rates for certain clients and overloading partners with day-to-day work to reinforce the relationship on other accounts. The best way of breaking the old habit is to start with the fee-capacity optimization plan we have already gone through. This sets important standards such as charge-out rates and utilization targets by professional level. Detailed allocation planning, particularly where many people's time is split across a multitude of small accounts, can be facilitated with the use of allocation spreadsheets. These are pretty simple but markedly absent in many PSFs (Figure 6.5).

The challenge with allocation is that it occurs at the client and account level, not at the office level. The decision about whom to allocate to an account will be based on a judgement about how much of a person's time at a specified billing rate a client will want. It will also be based on the complexity of the work that needs to be done and the degree of high-level advisory input required. The choice of professionals will also, of course, be

Employee code	Charge out rate/hour	Hours Client code					Billed hours	Un-billed client hours	Utili-zation % (1)	Target utili-zation	Variance %	Over-runs %	Target over-runs %	Variance %
		101	102	103	104	105								
101	230	14	21	3	10	26	70	4	74	50	48	5	5	0
102	60	2	0	0	14	58	68	6	74	100	-26	8	5	-60
103	180	16	14	18	0	0	47	1	48	60	-20	2	5	60
Total	Average	32	35	21	24	84	62	4	65	73	-11	5	5	0
	Target	30	31	21	20	81								
	Variance %	6	13	0	20	4								

▨ = problem area

① Based on 100/hour period as example

Figure 6.5 *Illustrative simplified allocation planning and evaluation sheet for a PSF using fees*

conditioned by the personality fit with the client. All these issues are client-specific. By contrast, the setting of utilization targets, billing rates and the professional structure are all set on an office- or firmwide basis. The trick is working from these broad parameters and converting them into something workable at the client level.

The problem in this conversion process from office to client level is that most PSFs fail to measure their economic performance at the client or project level. A PSF that fails to measure its economic performance at the client or project level will tend not to be able to optimize its overall performance since it won't know which clients and which of their respective projects drive the overall profit numbers. This means it will never be sure if it has staffed the account properly, how the account is affecting the firm's overall utilization numbers and whether it is really charging a full effective rate per hour. The profile of a typical PSF in terms of client contribution to profitability is illustrated in Figure 6.6. The usual pattern is a diminishing curve, with a small group of highly profitable clients and a long tail-end of underperformers. This implies that many PSFs are as bad at managing

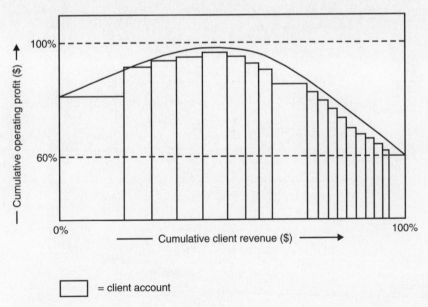

Figure 6.6 *Illustrative cumulative operating profit contribution of clients in a typical PSF*

their performance at an account level as they are at setting their fee capacity at an office level. Much of the rest of this book will focus its energies where the real action is—the client account.

PULLING IT ALL TOGETHER

As with all firms, financials just tell you about outcomes. They don't tell you how to get to a result. Having said that, many PSFs don't even bother to apply the rigour of financial measurement we have covered and they don't tend to analyse themselves on an optimization basis. While most PSFs will have an CFO, few will have a COO[1] who takes an operating perspective on how to achieve financial outcomes by influencing the way work is done and resource is deployed. Many will not prepare three-year plans and decisions will tend to be opportunistic, driven by the twists and turns of their clients. As a result, to date there have not been any standard financial frameworks for analysing how to maximize value creation in the peculiar case of the people business.

---

[1] COO = Chief Operating Officer.

7
Identifying Whether a PSF is Positioned to Maximize Returns to Shareholders

So how do you understand whether a professional service firm is positioned to achieve high returns, and whether it is extracting the most it could from its client activity to maximize shareholder value? As with any firm, there are a wide number of drivers of PSF performance, including the cyclical impact of changes in the overall economy. The issue is what levers do PSFs have at their disposal to influence their performance in given market conditions and how effectively do they utilize them. The six key levers available to the management of any PSF are illustrated in the Professional Service Model (PSM) in Figure 7.1:

- Client strategy
- Service mix
- Pricing strategies
- Process efficiency and internal structures
- Recruitment, incentives and career management
- Financial and process control

There is, of course, a delicate interdependence between this set of levers. Most PSFs fall down on a number of them or are not sufficiently aware of what can be done to improve their utilization of them. One reason for this is that the CEOs of most PSFs tend to be professionals whose background is outstanding client handling, not necessarily running a company to maximum

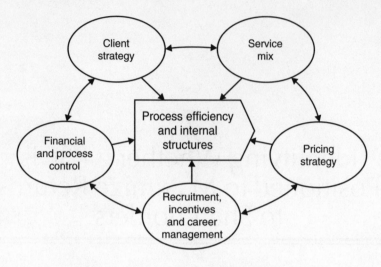

Figure 7.1   *The generic Professional Service Model*

effectiveness. Although relatively commonsensical, it is unusual to find a PSF achieving a balanced approach to the PSM. It is through the application of this basic set of principles that holding firms such as Omnicom, Interpublic and WPP are able to add dramatic shareholder value to the private companies they acquire.

CLIENT STRATEGY

The only thing a PSF is there to do is to service client needs. Naturally therefore the primary driver of the performance of any PSF is the effectiveness of its client acquisition and servicing strategy.

Clients come in every shape and size. Picking target customers is more important for a PSF than it is for any consumer goods manufacturer. Client targeting means a PSF gets to know that type of client really well, can predict their needs, that they make these clients aware of what the firm has to offer and that they have done work for clients like them before. Client targeting is more important for PSFs than for consumer goods firms because of the typical weighting of single clients in a PSF's overall revenue portfolio and hence their reliance on forming good partnerships that will endure. It is also important because of the heavy costs associated with new business pitches, the devastating costs of picking clients who don't pay properly and the profit benefit of long-term relationships .

It is also important that a PSF is choosy about which clients it picks because one client will have fundamentally different profit potential from another. This will be driven by their differing service expectations and their willingness to accept competitive charge-out rates. It will also be conditioned by their prospective longevity or how much farming potential they hold which, in turn, will be driven by the competitive position of the client itself in its own market. A PSF with weak clients will itself probably be weak.

Many PSFs are forced to make choices between significant clients because of "conflict issues"[1] (although the significance of the conflict issue varies segment by segment). They therefore have to choose carefully. It is also essential for profitability that a PSF has a decent hit to "pitch"[2] ratio. The way of maximizing this ratio is to know the client well and thereby ensure that any new projects that come up are awarded either without a pitch or with a high probability of winning. If a PSF picks the wrong client, they can find the business up for pitch to all competitors on a regular basis. If they choose the right one, their need to pitch competitively will fall and their margin will increase correspondingly.

The choice of client will also dictate the professional development of the firm. A client serviced for two years or more will typically drive the evolution of a different set of skills which, in turn, will influence the ability of the firm to win different sorts of clients and hire different sorts of professionals. The choice of client is much like a Las Vegas marriage—it has to be made in expectation of lasting forever but with the probability of lasting only years, most importantly, the choice of cient has to be made in full understanding that whatever else happens the professional life of the firm will not be the same afterwards.

The PSF that is flagging will typically have a very poorly

---

[1] Conflict means that, by virtue of having one client in a particular sector, the PSF will effectively be barred from taking on another in the same sector because the client will refuse to let their business be handled if there is any conflict of interest.

[2] "Pitch" is the generic term used in many PSFs for presentations for bids.

thought-through client strategy. They may have a vague sense of what clients they are pursuing, responding to notifications of pitch opportunities on a reactive basis with little discrimination about the potential client, its culture or its likely problems. They will typically rely on a lot of "cold-calling" to generate client leads. They will also tend to have assembled a group of generalists who are bright enough to turn their hand to anything as long as the client doesn't realize that they're learning on the back of the client itself (e.g. "borrowing his watch to tell him the time . . . "). Such firms will tend to suffer very high pitch-to-revenue costs and stumble from one short-term client assignment to another with very high single-client dependence at any one point in time. Their ability to grow consistently will continually be undermined by client upheavals. They will also typically suffer higher than average staff turnover due to disruptive account situations. The impact on their margins will be clear.

So what constitutes a good client strategy? There are a few key indicators that tell a lot about how well a firm has thought through who it services:

- Client concentration
- Farming performance
- Client specialization

Client Concentration

The typical weakness of many PSFs is excessive client concentration. As a rough rule of thumb, concentration means the top client accounting for more than 20% of fee income and/or the top three clients accounting for in excess of 50% of fee income. This can occur for good reasons; namely the development of the business off the back of a couple of client relationships sustained for years through superb service. More often, however, it is not so calculated.

Sometimes, the level of concentration is simply not seen as a problem since many large clients are collections of different clients or buying points within a single organization, giving the impression of low dependency on a single relationship. But, of course, the exposure to the vagaries of a single firm are still there.

The more worrying reasons for client concentration tend to be opportunism and poor management. A single relationship can materialize from nowhere and for a period allow full staff utilization. The firm just kicks back, takes the cash while it is flowing and invests behind it. Then the client moves on. The problem with opportunism is that it leads to erratic revenue growth and instability among the professional base. It also allows for little accumulation of specialized knowledge. In short, it is not a strategy at all.

The most damaging thing about concentration is that the natural imbalance between the negotiating power of the client and PSF tends to get further exaggerated. As soon as it becomes apparent that the PSF has nowhere else to turn, the client can begin to put pressure on prices, insist on audits of margins[3] and assimilate the value-added advisory pieces of the service into its own organization, reducing the PSF to the status of a standard supplier. This is the position some medium-size advertising agencies find themselves in when they are "conflicted out" of working for multiple clients in the same sector. McKinsey, by contrast, has successfully maintained its independent discretion to work for whom it likes. Indeed, it attracts clients based on its penetration of certain industrial sectors—clients don't want to be left out of the McKinsey club!

The other key effect of concentration is the deleterious impact it has on the professional quality of the firm. Good people quickly get bored working for one client year in and year out. One of the great things about the PSF environment is the exposure it provides to a wide variety of client situations. This is why people tend to migrate from clients into their PSF providers. If a firm relies on one client for a couple of years or more it will typically be unable to retain its best people or attract the best people. The result is a slow deterioration of the firm's professional standards and an inability to win new clients to reduce its dependency. This is the dependency death-spiral of the PSF.

The financial numbers can be misleading in the early stages of concentration. Like a drug addiction, the symptoms are rosy at first. The firm will typically be able to staff the account with lower-paid people as it gets more settled and familiar with the

---

[3] A number of specialist firms have emerged advising clients on PSF remuneration structures which almost invariably results in a lowering of margins for the PSF.

client. It will also be able to amortize client acquisition costs fully. It may even slow down its new business drive, further pushing down costs. These things will all help to buoy up the margins of the firm even when the underlying profitability of the account is on a longer-term downward curve. Then, of course, the profitability of the firm will decline and, if the client walks, will suddenly fall off a cliff.

A highly competitive PSF will tend to work to maintain the largest client at under 20% of revenue on an annualized basis although this may not hold on a monthly or quarterly basis as workloads shift. It will extract maximum charge-out rates from a strong negotiating position and retain the discretion to work for competitors of the client by deploying "Chinese walls". If there is a situation of client conflict which drives the need for global alignment with a single client, it will only do so on highly attractive contract terms. Figure 7.2 illustrates the typical relationship between sustained concentration ratios and the operating profits of a PSF.

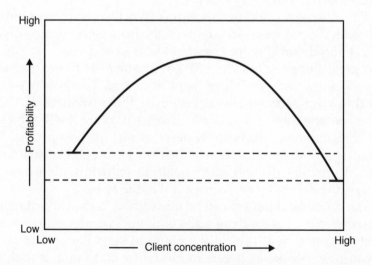

Figure 7.2 *Illustrative relationship between sustained client concentration and profitability in a PSF*

Farming Performance

The second key indicator of the quality of a PSF's client strategy is its ability to farm revenues. The percentage of a firm's revenue that comes from clients held for more than two years will directly correlate to its level of profitability. The key driver of this enhanced profitability is the fact that client relationships have "time economies", the counterpart of industry's "scale economies". The longer a client relationship, the lower the notional annual charge for acquisition amortization (it is notional because it will have to be expensed immediately), the greater the ability of the firm to spot new internal revenue sources which can be won at low cost, the more efficient the internal working process and the better the ability to deliver product right first time. Figure 7.3 illustrates the relationship between "time economies" and profitability.

Farming, of course, is the close relative of concentration. But it does not have the vices of concentration. Effective farming requires investment in a current client situation in order to yield new assignments. It cannot be borne out of harvesting which is

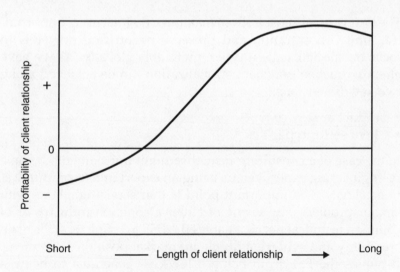

Figure 7.3 *Illustrative relationship between the longevity and profitability of a major client relationship for a PSF*

the usual approach associated with client concentration. Firms which are not effective farmers go through high client turnover and truncated revenue cycles. This makes effective budgeting and resource management extremely difficult to accomplish, further exaggerating the impact on profitability. In such situations, these firms tend to focus maniacally on winning new clients and get locked into the PSF death cycle of spiralling costs and diminishing margins. The key to PSF profitability is farming, not hunting.

Instinctively, most PSFs focus on acquisition—it's sexy, exciting and gets lots of press coverage. Few calculate the costs. Nor do many focus on average client retention rates or managing the volume of repeat revenues. For any potential purchaser of a PSF business, the key number they will look at is the size of the new business target necessary to hit budget. The larger this new business "plug" in the budget, the less trust they will be able to place in it. This is why strictly project-based businesses are fundamentally less attractive than long-term relationship based businesses.

Client Specialization

The best way for most PSFs to maximize their farming opportunity, limit concentration and preserve negotiating power is to focus on specialist client types, preferably globally. As we have already touched on, client specialization can be achieved along two key dimensions:

- Product or service type
- Client sector type

In the case of a consulting firm, this might translate into being a re-engineering expert versus being an expert in telecommunications clients. The important point is that servicing clients with similar problems, by virtue of either a common industry or of common technical needs, enables the PSF to refine its skills, gain credibility and achieve a dominant market position in its niche. It moves the PSF from being a low-cost generalist to being a high-margin differentiator which is the only viable position for a PSF.

A weak PSF will usually have its portfolio of clients both concentrated and spread across a large number of sectors at the margins. The result is failure to gain critical mass or reputation in any particular market, typically losses on business in marginal sectors and failure to develop first-class professional expertise in any one area (Figure 7.4). Typically firms fall into this generalist trap through opportunistic pursuit of any client leads, almost without discrimination. Even if such a firm appears successful at a given point in time, its earnings performance will typically be fragile and its position with its key clients vulnerable to attack by focused specialists.

Many of the large generalist PSFs have overcome this risk by establishing specialist practice areas within the general firm. In this context, the umbrella PSF has effectively become a provider of an umbrella brand and back-office services to a grouping of multi-specialist teams. This is the dominant strategy of the Big Six accountancy practices spinning off their M&A and computer consulting groups as separate operating

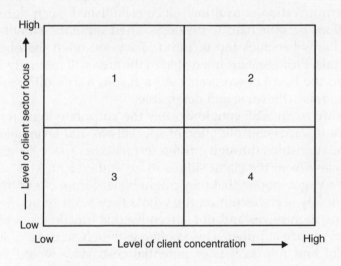

1 = most profitable
4 = least profitable

Figure 7.4   *Illustrative relationship between sector focus and
client concentration for a typical PSF*

units who assiduously guard their independence. The theory is good—exploit the economies and client referral opportunities available through breadth, along with the benefits of developing sectorally or technically focused sets of skills. But it also carries risks. It can be hard for clients to believe the firm is committed to its own sector or its own specialist problem when it is clear that the umbrella brand is operating across another twenty industry sectors with thirty other products and trying to refer clients between groups to maximize revenue. It is also hard to re-create the professional commitment of a specialist in a generalist group. Having said that, the Big Six have done pretty damn well out of this strategy!

The best firms are often purist, exploiting their specialist knowledge globally on the coat tails of global clients. Firms such as Carabina have focused on expanding event management globally through acquisition and achieved a tremendous market valuation as a result. The Maritz Group has remained firmly concentrated on executive rewards and motivational consulting. IMG and ISL have remained tightly focused on sports management and sponsorship. Hay and Towers Perrin have specialized on remuneration consulting. Once established, such dominant positions become hard to dislodge. Their reputation among target clients becomes top of mind. They are often the object of referrals. Professionals interested in the area will naturally gravitate to the best-known brand. As a result, a true differentiated position is achievable and defensible.

Inside many PSF conglomerates the corporate logic remains firmly towards consolidation of specialisms and leverage of client relationships through cross-referral across specialist groups. The view from the client side is more ambivalent. Most clients have a vague notion that they might benefit from closer integration of key services but on the whole they want to do the integrating themselves and not surrender this function to a professional service supplier. This is often as much an issue of loss of control and role as it is of potential cost. Why would a chief financial officer want his accountancy firm also to manage his acquisitions programme? There would be nothing left for him to do!

From the professional standpoint the natural momentum is probably away from integration. This is largely just a territorial (and very human) issue. You only need look as far as the Andersen Consulting/Arthur Andersen schism or the tensions between units in groups such as Cordiant which have driven the process of de-merger. The typical expression of this professional tension is the splitting away of specialist groups from the generalist host company. Bain Management Consultants has been the "victim" of a large number of these over the past ten years. Spectrum, a small UK telecomms consultancy, is an already successful, highly specialist McKinsey spin-off. The PSF conglomerates are periodically reminded of the error of overriding this natural tendency towards specialization by seismic splits. The Saatchi & Saatchi empire was first stalled on the rock of acquiring a remuneration consultancy business, Hay, in the vain hope of allying it with advertising. Groups such as Omnicom, Interpublic and WPP have thrived, by contrast, by preserving the individual specialist brands of the firms they have acquired and ensuring that all brands are tightly clustered within marketing communications.

Specialism is king, multi-specialism is viable and integration or bundling is the holy grail but, given the tremendous difficulty of pulling it off, almost certainly the toughest strategy in the long run for the average player and the most prone to unravelling.

Pulling It All Together

PSFs which show little coherence in their client base will be far less competitive in the medium term than firms that have coherent client bases. The interesting thing is that the majority of PSFs show a relatively low degree of client strategy, growing on the basis of opportunism. This means that there is a large amount of value that can be created by PSFs as they focus and globalize.

PSFs typically have a portfolio of clients that make a mixed contribution to company performance (refer back to Figure 6.6, p. 77). The classic bad client strategy is to try to restore profitability by cutting off the underperforming tail of clients. The problem with this hatchet approach is that unless overhead can be removed at the same rate, the effect will simply be to depress the margins on the remaining accounts. As a result, most PSFs are very much stuck with the client base they have acquired, which makes choosing the right ones in the first place all the more important.

At the present moment there are only a handful of PSF sectors which have evolved into global specialist networks. A few have begun to hit the mature part of the life cycle, such as auditing. For the bulk of PSFs the specialist growth curve is still ahead of them, primarily through client sector focus. PSFs have yet to discover the concept of "core competencies"[4] much as they have yet to discover process re-engineering and TQM[5] as we will come onto. This means that there is one thing you can say for sure about PSFs—there is still money on the table!

SERVICE MIX

The counterpart of client strategy is product or service strategy. As we have discussed, most PSFs have a choice of specializing by product or by client sector. Hay, for example, focuses on client remuneration issues but services every client sector imaginable. The Piper Trust in the UK, by contrast, focuses both on consulting and venture capital services solely for the retail trade. PSFs which specialize both sectorally and by service tend to be niche players with limited absolute growth opportunities. Hence the thrust for most larger PSFs is to take one route or the other (Figure 7.5).

The sector route and service route to specialization are very different strategies. Service specialization has always been the classic route for development of PSFs seeking to extend themselves on a global basis. The results are most of the familiar global names in the PSF business such as J. Walter Thompson in advertising, Coopers & Lybrand in accountancy and Clifford Chance in legal services. Service specialization is premised on the idea that the finite commodities are specialist skills and proprietary methods.

However, this is not always the most defensible position. Intellectual frameworks cannot be registered and most services

---

[4] "Core competencies" is the in-vogue term to describe those areas of activity in which the firm can genuinely call itself expert and able to differentiate itself.
[5] TQM = total quality management, a philosophy guiding the management of the internal processes of a firm.

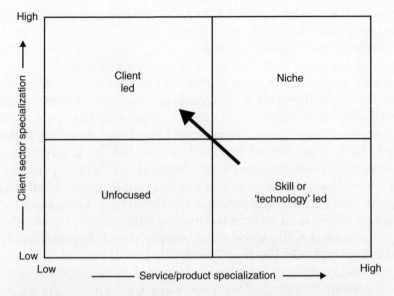

Figure 7.5 *Illustrative strategies for specialization in generic PSF segments*

tend to reach maturity very quickly—it took only five years for BPR to become an established technique practiced by a multitude of consultancies despite having been "pioneered" by CSC Index. The technical entry barriers to most PSF sectors are not high and the equivalent to R&D tends not to be in the domain of private companies but controlled by institutions such as the Harvard Business School and Wharton. Service specialism does give firms an advantage but only as long as it is not based solely on methodologies. Rather, it has to be invested in the brand and the people and subject to a continual process of organic renewal.

The finite commodity in PSFs are client relationships and client knowledge, not technology or methodology. The only defensible thing PSFs have is a great relationship with a set of clients and a level of understanding of clients and their industries that make the PSF indispensable. The strongest relationships tend to be built when PSFs have an excellent general understanding of the issues facing a client and fashion their services to meet those needs rather than continuing to remorselessly sell them the same solution to different problems. The power of PSFs is to customize, not to mass market. Probably the best way of acquiring this level of understanding is to know the client's sector as well or better than the client does herself.

Sector competence tends to be a virtuous circle. Because a PSF sees all the firms in the sector, it becomes invaluable as a source of information about other players. As this knowledge deepens, so its hold on the firms in a sector tends to tighten. A firm such as McKinsey, for example, will tend to work for all the firms in the financial services sector. Because its knowledge about the sector is broader than any of its clients alone, it is in a very strong bargaining position *vis-à-vis* any single client. Not surprisingly, the foundation stone service of a consulting firm specializing by sector will tend to be competitor benchmarking. The more competent a PSF is at benchmarking, whether or not it sells this information directly to clients or simply uses it to condition its offering, typically the more profitable it will be and the more defensible will be its position.

It is likely that the real winners over the next few years will be those firms that manage to migrate from being "product" specialists in the traditional mould to being sector specialists or multi-sector specialists. This is the ground many of the global holdings have straddled by buying up strong independent brands. As client sector specialization becomes a dominant organizational model, firms relying on old product-led specialisms, such as general strategy consulting or general audit, will find themselves increasingly outflanked. The challenge facing generalist firms will be to accommodate quasi-independent specialists within their own organizations in a form of confederation rather than swallow them up in the name of cross-referral and synergy.

PRICING STRATEGIES

The pricing strategy a PSF pursues will determine not only its profitability but also its positioning in the market. In an industry governed by client perceptions about what is being received, the premium a firm can command is a direct indication of the value of the service to the client and of the market position of the firm.

In most industrial settings firms have a clear choice—either to compete on low costs and low prices or to differentiate and sustain high prices. Both strategies are equally viable depending on the industry and can result in similar margin levels. In most PSF segments this stark choice does not exist in the same way. It is usually not viable for PSFs to try to compete on price alone. Since the primary cost is people, reduction in the cost base to accommodate lower price points quickly erodes the professional quality of the firm. The first signs of this are overleveraging of partners (e.g. increasing the ratio of partners to non-partners to a point where leadership is diluted away) as the firm attempts to lower the average direct salary mix on assignments while preserving the average billing rate. The effect of this, of course, is that the firm's growth begins to slow as its partners are unable to feed the great machine they have created with enough assignments to keep it moving forward and quality deteriorates.

Some PSF sectors have made the collective error of allowing price to become a primary purchase criterion by allowing clients to enforce bidding for contracts on price instead of competence. This has usually been exacerbated in these areas by oversupply of services. The pitch-ridden environment of small-scale, local advertising and the tendering process in government IT contracts are two obvious examples.

Most healthy PSFs in healthy segments compete on quality and not price. Their main focus is achieving high enough levels of value added to sustain higher salaries than competitors and hence maintain the best professional talent. Most PSFs competing on the basis of value added can make a healthy profit and the very best can achieve super-profits even after compensating their professionals far higher than their client counterparts. Differentiation is the only viable strategy for the successful PSF.

Value Pricing

With this fact in mind, it should not be surprising that the most profitable pricing strategy for PSFs is "value pricing". Value pricing involves giving a single price for a discrete deliverable or defined process which reflects the value the firm believes it brings to the client rather than reflecting the underlying cost of delivering it. Defining this value is often hard and, because of the intangible nature of the product, cannot always easily be tied to a tangible and measurable benefit by the client. The result is that setting the pricing usually relies on the PSF's own sense of the tradable value of its service and what value it could extract from offering the same service to a competitor client. The PSF has to have "balls" and a somewhat arrogant sense of its own worth to pull it off. It also needs a good brand and outstanding professionals. That is why value pricing is usually limited to those firms that dominate the top end of their PSF segment such as McKinsey or Goldman Sachs.

The great thing about value pricing is that it severs the strangling umbilical cord tying price to cost. This means that the firm is free to adjust its cost base as it sees fit without disclosing its underlying cost information to the client. The shrewd firms will highly leverage senior partners with heavy use of young foot soldiers to lower their cost base on the account while maintaining premium pricing. The result can be super-profits provided that professional quality is sufficiently well maintained to preserve the perceived value of the brand. They can also ensure that they use lots of bought-in services which they can mark up.

Rather than referring itself to the cost of delivery, value pricing will usually link itself to a client benefit. An investment bank, for example, will charge a client a percentage of the value of a deal for M&A advisory work. A consultant might take a percentage of costs saved in a client reorganization as a result of their BPR work. An accounting firm might take equity in a client for advice during a restructuring rather than fees. All achieve a pricing structure divorced from the cost of delivery and linked to the economic value of the transaction for the client.

One mitigating feature of this pricing strategy from the client's standpoint is that the actual cost of the service to them tends to be small in comparison to the collateral which is bought as a result of the advice. Most advertising agencies receive between 12% and 14% of the value of the media bought; most investment banks get around 1–3% of the value of an M&A deal completed on behalf of a client depending on the size of the deal. Such value pricing arrangements also seem to bind together the financial interests of the PSF and the interests of the client in getting the transaction completed, rather than yielding hourly fees for the PSF based on how protracted the process becomes. It is also far easier for the client to manage a simple ratio than to administer a more complex fee arrangement.

From the PSF side, value pricing does not come without risks (that is why it is potentially highly lucrative). Its risks stem precisely from the fact that this payment formula has nothing to do with the work a PSF has put in. This is fine as long as prices remain high relative to cost. But if, over time, prices have been allowed to fall due to competitive pressure but professional costs have crept up, then the equation can unravel. The pricing, for example, might have been set in the past based on a calcula-tion of the average historical workload. If this pricing formula has just become a habit, these assumptions may no longer hold true. The result is a disjunct between pricing and the cost of delivery which will leave the firm exposed to the break-even function illustrated in Figure 7.6. Of course, if the client's expen-diture on the collateral is far greater than the workload then the PSF makes super-profits. If the opposite is true then it can make dramatic losses. It therefore systematically increases the volatil-ity of the earnings of the PSF, obeying the inexorable law relating risk and return.

The term often used for a historically established value pric-ing formula is "commission". Commission is typically ex-pressed as a percentage of the collateral bought, whether this is the cost of media space bought in the case of an advertising

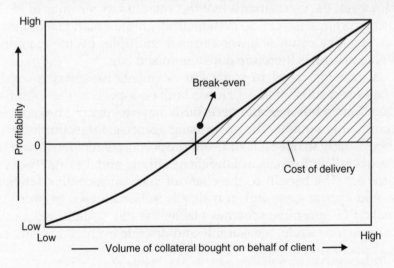

Figure 7.6 *Illustrative economics of a commission-based remuneration system*

agency or the value of a deal in the case of an investment bank. In any commission situation the PSF is free to adjust their cost base in a way that they cannot do with hourly fees. They can manage down their workload with the client and optimize their time with pristine accuracy without lowering prices to induce a superb margin.

The problem for most firms operating on a commission is that the commission rates have slowly fallen over time and the resource requirements have stayed the same or increased due to competition for talented people. Because of the lucrativeness of their pricing system, such PSFs tend to have little culture of time management. The result is that the only way they have of defending their margins as commission rates fall tends to be to employ cheaper people and invest less. The result is a downward spiral of standards and a slowly declining commission rate as the primary purchase criterion of the client becomes cost. Sectors such as advertising, for example, are in some places suffering the consequences of a commission rate system set up thirty years ago.

Some PSF sectors have fought their way out of this dilemma while sticking with commission. The investment banks, for example, have done this by introducing variable commissions depending on the size of the deal, such as the Lehman Scale[6]. However, the fact remains that the volatility in earnings of PSFs using commission can be systematically higher than that of firms on fees. The result is lower earnings multiples by the markets. Value pricing is therefore not an unmixed bag.

A growing trend in some PSF segments has been towards "pay-for-results" (PFR). PFR has built on aspects of the commission system but does not necessarily have its pricing linked to a commodity bought. The advertising agencies, for example, tend increasingly to have a significant proportion of income linked to the overall performance of the client's brand and the quality of its product. The benefit to the client of such an incentive scheme would appear great but in reality is not unalloyed. In order to make PFR incentive schemes viable, the PSF usually has to tie them to a concrete, measurable and discrete event. Acquisitions

---

[6] The Lehman Scale is a scale for remuneration on deals developed by Lehman Brothers, the investment bank, which increases the commission as the size of the deal falls.

and cost-reduction exercises which fall straight to the bottom line fit the bill. PSFs collect immediately since causality is fairly easy to demonstrate. Revenue growth activities and business improvement activities usually do not have these characteristics. Causality is tough to prove and client benefits will probably be delayed, making it hard for the PSF to collect. This means that incentive fees are often only associated with cost reduction and deal making-type exercises, neither of which may be in the long-term interest of the client. The behaviour they promote among PSFs can therefore be quite dysfunctional in certain situations.

Fees

The usual pricing structure of the mature PSF segments is to tie the price of the service to the cost of delivery. The most common mechanism of doing this is the professional hourly fee. Hourly fees are usually calculated by level of employee based on a banding of the employees within the firm. Hourly fees will typically include both direct costs and a charge for overhead as well as a calculated operating margin (Figure 7.7). Assuming that these rates are calculated correctly, and the overhead charge assumes an achievable level of overall professional utilization,[7] the firm should hit a target margin automatically. That's the theory at least.

Of course, things don't work that simply in practice. The trouble with quoted fee rates for the PSF is that they create a high degree of market transparency. Most clients, having been presented to at pitches by multiple PSFs, will know what the average rates and spread of rates are by level of professional. They will also have a keen sense for which types of professionals they want on their business. Most competitors will also have a sense of the market hourly rates of the other firms in the sector. The result is that most firms will pitch in at what they perceive to be a competitive rate, usually resulting in a shift of the mean rate for the sector to what is effectively the lowest price.

---

[7] The overhead charge will not only include real overhead such as office space but also the cost of unallocated, uncharged professional time which has to be absorbed by the accounts serviced by the firm.

Level	Average direct costs/hr ①	Average overhead allocation/hr ②	Target operating margin (%)	Implied fee rate ($/hr)	Average market rate
1	130	85	10	240	230
2	50	33	30	108	100
3	15	10	50	38	40
Average	65	43	30	129	124

① Assumes 240 days a year and 8 hours a day

② Based on direct costs, including an allocation of unbilled staff costs due to less than 100% utilization/billability

Figure 7.7   *Illustrative calculation of charge-out rates for a generic PSF*

Of course, as long as the firm has calculated its rates carefully, including realistic utilization targets, and manages its allocation of resource and monitoring of time well, then it will make money. The problems occur for those firms who are unable to do these things well. Fee-pricing mechanisms work well for firms who understand how to set them and manage their time and cost effectively in order to fulfil their utilization assumptions. They are disasters for those who don't.

Among fee-based businesses there will typically be a minority of firms who are able to manage these variables with effectiveness and hence price accurately. Put simply, they will keep a realistic and tight link between pricing and costs in order to achieve a decent margin. The bad ones will not do the planning and management necessary. They will gravitate towards the lowest market rate, focus on maintaining high utilization among all professionals and then disappear into an unprofitable downward pricing spiral. In this situation, the pricing and the costs tend to become uncoupled and disaster to ensue.

Interestingly, the firms which are able to value price tend to be similar to these poorly performing fee-based firms in terms of their laxity of cost and time management. They tend not to keep time sheets, do not place an internal value on their time and staff accounts solely by feel and fit. Of course, the difference is that their professional quality allows them to do so profitably because they can charge enough to create a thick cushion.

Often, the most turbulent situation is in sectors where firms are used to value pricing but where fee-type arrangements are creeping in because of commoditization of the product and rationalization of suppliers by clients. Many local, medium-size firms in the advertising industry, for example, are accustomed to being paid a commission based on the value of media space bought. Agencies are not used to managing time very well (hence the apocryphal advertising lunches!). Fees put the premium on efficient management and process, not brilliance or creativity, and this is not an agency forté. This is why accounting firms work effectively with fees but agencies tend not to. Have you ever tried to get a "creative" to keep a timesheet?

So How Should a PSF Price?

Different pricing decisions will directly influence the firm's fee capacity and will dramatically alter the profitability of the firm. They will drive its professional structure, utilization and development since they drive the ability of the firm to achieve competitive salary levels. Therefore pricing decisions are among the most important a PSF has to make. Given this, it is quite surprising how little attention the typical PSF CEO gives to their pricing strategy. In fact, it would not be an exaggeration to say that usually they have no pricing strategy at all.

The winning strategy is pretty simple—charge-out on a value basis and manage internally as if the firm were charging on a fee basis. This means, as far as pricing is concerned, the PSF will have severed the suffocating link between price and costs, allowing charge-out rates to rise as the firm can lay claim to increasing value added by building its reputation. It means, however, that it will manage itself internally as if the link between costs and price were still there, usually by means of an internal charge-out rate system. This strategy is surprisingly rare and relies on a strong client franchise. But it is not complicated to manage, as we will come onto presently.

Pulling It All Together

The next decade will witness an increasing polarization of pricing strategies. At one end will be those firms that are able to value price by virtue of their superior understanding of particular client sectors and their command of particular skills-sets. At the other end of the spectrum will be those firms stuck with poor commission-based systems which they are unable to break out of because of market rigidity and unfamiliarity with fees. For such firms costs and income will increasingly get out of whack. Then, between these two extremes, there will be the vast majority of fee-based companies who will vary in performance according to their ability to manage their professional resources, budget effectively and value their time (Figure 7.8). It is in this vast middle ground that PSFs will have to go down the process learning-curve that industry has been down over the last decade. The archetypal outward-facing industry will have to turn in on itself—something most PSFs will be uncomfortable doing!

PROCESS EFFICIENCY AND INTERNAL STRUCTURES

A key driver of the profitability of PSFs is their ability to manage the process of delivering outstanding client service with maximum efficiency. As with a manufacturer, the efficiency of the process and the quality of the output are highly correlated. If it costs the firm a lot to deliver a project it will almost always be because it has not delivered what the client wants to an acceptable standard first time. This will result in rework and revisions, the counterpart of a factory's scrap rate and customer reject rate. It will also result in delays which always damage a client relationship because professional services are almost always highly time sensitive.

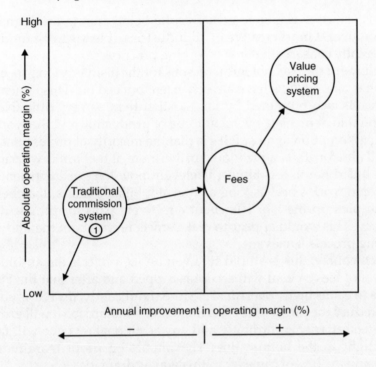

① Based on historical commission rates

Figure 7.8 *Illustrative generic pricing strategies for PSFs*

Despite its importance, the concept of "process" is pretty much an alien one in the PSF industry. Manufacturing has been through the wringer of the quality movements and assimilated concepts such as Kaizen, statistical process control, JIT[8] and TQM as a matter of necessity. The process movement, reborn in its latest reincarnation "re-engineering", has also fundamentally transformed approaches to the way work is managed. This has resulted in tremendous productivity improvements among industrials and service businesses over the past ten years and a far more rigorous approach to assessing efficiency. The professional service industry, by contrast, has not really changed in a process

[8] JIT, or just-in-time, is an approach to manufacturing which avoids the accumulation of inventory and relies on highly efficient synchronization of different stages of the production process.

sense since it was invented. Despite being among the highest growth and most creative of all industries, it tends to be fundamentally conservative in its working practices.

Some of the psychological reasons for the disinterest in process issues among PSFs have already been touched on. This nonchalance is also promoted by the fact that there is very little fixed capital to depreciate over a volume of production and the working assumption in most PSFs is that the majority of professionals will aim for 100% utilization. Furthermore, if the firm is working on billed hours it is almost irrelevant how long or inefficiently people work since, as long as they are billable hours, the client will pick up the tab. The client effectively pays for the inefficiency. This would appear to make any concern about the underlying process irrelevant.

Of course, this is stupidity. Even on fee projects the absolute level of fees a client will accept is capped and after that the PSF has to eat its own "overruns".[9] More significantly, if a PSF is able to reduce the direct time consumed on a standard job it will grow its fee capacity accordingly and any additional revenue will fall straight to the bottom line. The impact on profit margins of freeing up 10% of capacity in this way is dramatic.

Another reason the process movement hasn't taken hold is the culture of most PSFs. PSFs tend to be inhabited by individuals who take a very personal approach to generating ideas and delivering client value. The clients in turn will each tend to vary in the way they wish to see a project run. Their expectations of staffing levels will also vary, as will their demands for interaction between the PSF and their organization. The usual assumption is, therefore, that most PSFs are not typified by a single, repetitive process but rather a wide variation on a set of basic themes—customization overrules standards. This would appear to make process standardization not only difficult but usually counterproductive—clients and primadonna staff don't like it.

Accordingly, most PSFs are not managed on a process basis but rather on a "cost pool"[10] basis. The classic measures of

---

[9]   An overrun is the volume of time that professionals spend on an account which they cannot bill to the client as a percentage of the total time spent working on the account.

[10]   A cost pool approach to cost management is one in which costs are simply grouped by category, such as overhead, and then allocated out on a basis of a cost driver such as time.

performance such as the staff cost/revenue ratio are used to manage direct costs as a pool. As long as this ratio is low enough the assumption is that the underlying process on each account is reasonably efficient. Of course, what usually happens is that these ratios are set by industry standards, which typically reflect historical expectations and working methods. They do not really give any sense of whether the firm is optimizing its activities. What they do achieve is to save management the stress of delving into the inner workings of the firm in a systematic way.

If a typical PSF process differs from that of a manufacturer in that the PSF process tends not to be consistent over time or by client, this raises the issue of whether most PSFs should even attempt to manage to any standards the underlying activities of the firm. The answer is simply one of balance. Most PSFs leave a lot of potential value on the table by not focusing on the process by which they deliver service. The best demonstration of this is looking at the profitability by client and by project. Typically, profitability will vary dramatically on a client-by-client and project-by-project basis (refer back to Figure 6.6 p. 77), reflecting the underlying vagaries of ever-shifting processes on each client assignment.

The first problem most PSFs encounter in trying to move forward is that they have no idea what processes they follow and how these compare to performance benchmarks. The standard way of getting a handle on the process of a PSF is called "process mapping". Process mapping simply lays out the flow of work on an account and identifies the key activities which drive it. Figure 7.9 illustrates a generic process map for an advertising agency.

Process Mapping

So what do you do with a process map? The first cut is to distinguish between those activities that add visible client value and those which are back-room functions on an account. Figure 7.10 illustrates the client-visible and back-room activities for the generic advertising agency. It is usually possible to quantify the volume of client-facing versus non-client-facing work either in terms of number of tasks performed or, preferably, professional hours. Why worry about this distinction? Simple. In an industry

Account management	Planning and research	Creative	TV production	Media planning and buying
Receive client brief				
Crack client brief				
Present to client				
	Creative brainstorm			
		Create story board		
Rehearse presentation				
Present to client		Finalize mechanicals		
Choose director				
	Produce media plan			Produce media plan
Brief director			Brief director	
Internal approval			Internal approval	
Present to client				
Preproduction meeting			Preproduction meeting	Present plan to client
Sign and send to finance				Media plan approved
Preproduction meeting with client				
			Shoot	
Send copy to client				Book media space
				Invoice client
Send film to station				
Close job and invoice				

Figure 7.9 *Illustrative simplified process map for a generic advertising agency*

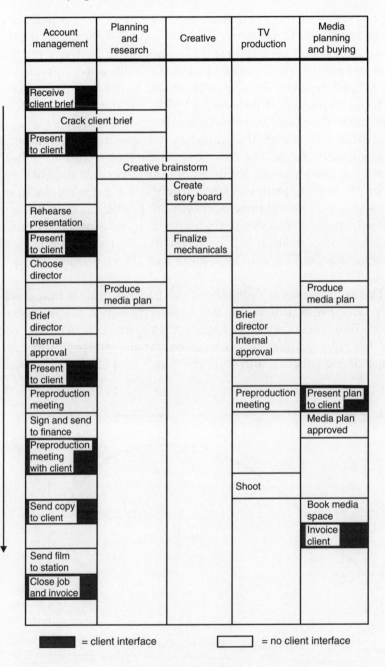

Figure 7.10   *Reconfigured simplified process map for a generic advertising agency showing areas of client interaction*

where much of the value is created through client contact and "face time", no firm wants to stay away from the client for too long. An excessively high ratio of "back-office" activity relative to client-facing activity is bad and as this ratio slides upwards so the billability and the client value-added of the firm declines.

To a certain degree it therefore holds true that a firm's ratio of internal to external functions correlates to its sustainable level of profitablity. However, this cannot be extrapolated *ad infinitum*. A firm's ability to do the less sexy, back-room stuff to a high standard will drive its ability to deliver premium product. For example, the analysts working largely behind the scenes in an investment bank will provide information which is invaluable to the salesperson convincing their clients to take positions in the markets. The relationship between the "activities ratio" and profitability will usually look more like the curve illustrated in Figure 7.11.

The second useful thing about the process map is that it will help you break down the firm's activities into discrete tasks much like the stages in a manufacturing process. Working out the average number of professional hours consumed at each stage of the process, and thus the direct cost absorbed by each

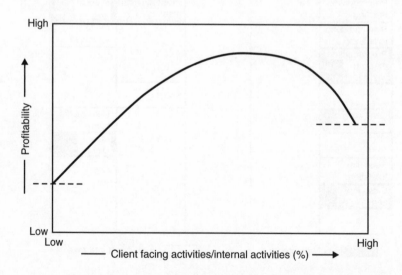

Figure 7.11   *Illustrative relationship between the volume of client-facing activities, internal activities and profitability for a generic PSF*

stage, enables one to understand where most resource is consumed. It also shows which pieces of the process have the longest throughput time[11] and which constitute bottle necks (Figure 7.12). This will help the PSF make informed decisions about whether more resource should be added in key areas of the process, whether certain stages should be charged for separately because of their cost or whether certain stages could be eliminated altogether.

Understanding the cost economics of the activities that go into delivering a service is only the first stage. The real challenge is to decide what drives these costs. In the case of our advertising agency, for example, the key drivers of the process tend to be the number of meetings held with the client and between departments, the extent of handovers of work between departments in order to produce a completed deliverable and the number of times the client demands rework. Understanding the process is only of value if it is used by a firm to see what drives its costs.

Typically few PSFs bother to break down their processes into tasks and do not understand which tasks drive their cost structure and their time to deliver. This means that their ability to both manage down-costs and fine-tune pricing is relatively low. PSFs can to some degree get away with it because most professionals are adaptable—they can turn their hand to different parts of the process or indeed follow it through from start to finish, jumping on problem areas when they arise. Most manufacturers, by contrast, rely on a set of specialized, dedicated machines and operators which are inflexible. This means that the resource pool in PSFs is far more flexible in responding to changing dynamics in the process as a result of changing client needs. However, by failing to understand the process and its economics, most PSFs leave a lot of value on the table.

Many PSF sectors have recently come under more pressure to push for efficiencies, particularly as their clients have been going through their own intense efficiency drives. This has resulted in

[11] Throughput time is either the calendar time it takes a PSF to complete a project or the staff time it absorbs in completing a project. In an industrial setting 'cycle time' is the key measure—cycle time is the time between two pieces falling off the end of the production line. In the PSF setting cycle time is not a relevant measure because the process is not sequential and staff work on multiple projects, each with different deadlines.

		Receive and process brief	Planners prepare consumer strategy	Creatives prepare creative strategy	Account management sell in concept	Media group buy media space	Full production ②
A	Number of professional hours ① available	1000	800	700	1300	400	300
B	Throughput time of brief ③	100	300	250	400	60	20
C	Potential output (A/B)	10	2.7	2.8	3.25	6.7	15
D	Actual output	3	3	3	3	3	3
E	Utilization (D/C) (%)	30	100	100	92	45	20

① Professional hours = number of professional x 240 days per year x 8 hours per day x underlying utilization target on client work

② Outsourced function

③ Throughput time = professional hours necessary to complete

⬚ = over-capacity   ▥ = bottlenecks

Figure 7.12   *Illustrative diagnosis of a simplified process for an advertising agency*

widespread experimentation with new organizational structures. For all firms, the 1990s has been the decade of process thinking—process re-engineering has meant a revolution, driving reorganization around the process rather than around traditional specialist functions. The prevalent expression of this idea has been the team. PSFs meanwhile are only just beginning to catch on!

Team Structures

Traditionally most PSFs have organized themselves along classical departmental lines, based on functional groups. The driving force behind this is the specialization of skills. In the traditional advertising agency, the creative dreaming up a wild campaign evolved a very different set of skills from the account manager having to argue about the pricing of a shoot. In the PSF setting this has usually meant department heads located on separate floors of a building, with their own hiring policies and work cultures. A client job would get thrown from one department silo over the wall into another. This has driven all the familiar role definitions—in the agency world this includes the account manager, the planner, the media buyer, the creative, the researcher, etc.

Over the last few years, the process movement has diagnosed this as a major driver of inefficiency, producing the culture of endless meetings, parochialism, slow throughput times and high error rates. The re-engineered vision is one of cross-functional client teams, seated together, working on a joint problem in real time. The team model was born in industrial settings but has now begun to be exported to the PSF world.

In team-based organizations, instead of working in their departments of like-minded people, professionals have been thrown into groups of people from a cross-section of functions. The basis of organization in such situations is usually the client itself. In such a structure, instead of reporting to a boss who is a copywriter born and bred, a creative might owe her loyalty to an account manager nurturing a particular soft drinks client (Figure 7.13).

Why teams? The theory is that work can flow more efficiently between a small group of people working cooperatively together than it can across departments with their own agendas. Problems can get ironed out instantaneously rather than through slow reiteration. Professionals feel more committed to contributing to a client outcome they can see. They have a greater sense of empowerment and ownership, particularly since team structures almost always imply dedication to specific clients. Often these teams are given full P&L responsibility, which means that they can be incentivized on the basis of

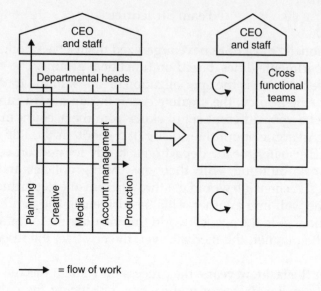

→ = flow of work

Figure 7.13   *Illustrative restructuring of departments in an advertising agency*

measurable economic performance. On the cost side, the expensive department heads, logistics managers and "traffic" people can be pruned. Also small teams tend to have less room for hierarchy and therefore the costs associated with the classical pyramid can be collapsed.

Whether these benefits are decisive is still questionable. It is early days for the team concept in PSFs. In the advertising world, for example, where there has been widespread experimentation with teams, there is scant evidence of the overwhelming benefits of team-based organization. The process itself of examining structure and streamlining can often be beneficial for the firm concerned, exposing dead wood and inefficiency. But it is a matter of debate whether the move to teams itself pays.

PSFs historically evolved department structures for a reason — the development and preservation of specialist skills. Intangible skills often quickly get eroded if they have no quality champion or protector. The loss of specialism can therefore quickly result in a loss of quality, particularly if department heads are fired. The associated role of departments is social. Like-minded people with similar skills and interests tend to gravitate to and operate best with like-minded people. It is the intensity of interaction between bright people which results in the birth of great ideas. And great ideas is all most PSFs have to offer! The best people tend to be attracted by the shining lights in their field, not by the efficiency of a firm's processes. Also, while most clients will show a concern about the efficiency of a PSF supplier, this will rank lower in the list of their purchase criteria than having access to the best thinking in the field. PSFs get fired for stale thinking or for taking the client for granted, not for being less than perfectly efficient (even if they don't maximize profits as a result!)

Department-based structures also have the benefit of flexibility. Whereas teams are usually client dedicated, people in departments tend to work on a wide number of projects at one time, lending specialist skills as part of the overall process on each client. In most PSFs such flexibility is essential as the workload on each individual client tends to modulate from month to month and much of the work is of a short-term, project nature. This means that structuring teams around specific clients is tough without creating patchy pieces of spare capacity in some groups and undercapacity in others on a month-by-month basis. The only way to avoid this is to trade capacity on a charged-out basis between teams which usually creates a seething bed of antagonisms. It is often unimplementable.

Most PSFs have responded to the productivity and process challenge by experimenting with new structural approaches. They have taken "restructuring" literally. The interesting question for most PSFs is whether structure is the relevant issue. It is not clear that tackling the problem from a purely structural perspective is the right way to go. Team structures are a crude response to the correct observations about many PSFs—the excessively long throughput time for much of the work, driven by laborious meetings between the departments, excessive time spent on non-client-facing tasks, and the failure to pin down accountability for the client deliverable. However, these shortcomings are usually better tackled through simpler means other than complete restructurings. They can also be tackled without losing the vital flexibility and professional quality achieved by departmental structures.

Accountability

So how should PSFs respond to the productivity challenge if not through changes in their structure? The underlying thrust of the more enlightened improvement processes among PSFs is usually to broaden the basis of profit accountability in the firm. The limitation with the old departmental approach is that profit responsibility only lies with the MD, aided by the FD and maybe a couple of other senior people. The weakness of this is an absence of profit control at the account level. It is this absence of accountability which produces the indifference to efficiency among people who can influence the process. This helps produce the familiar client profit contribution curve.

One of the tenets of the team system is that a single person becomes MD of each dedicated client group and has to manage their client relationships to make profit on their dedicated resource base (teams are usually most efficient around 14 people or $2 million of fee income). This means they have to focus on the process on their accounts. However, the same benefit can usually be derived from simply making the person running each account profit responsible within the traditional department framework. Combining account profit responsibility with the flexible resourcing pattern of departments is very powerful. It means that there is enough flexibility in deploying professionals across accounts to ensure that overall company capacity can be managed tightly, and that there is enough control at each revenue source to ensure that a decent level of profit is made on each and every piece of business (Figure 7.14).

Such an approach is not structural; it is based on the principle of giving people economic control and incentivizing them. Structural approaches to efficiency in PSFs are not usually the best route for the simple reason that the best PSFs are fluid environments where highly skilled people have to be deployed in ever-shifting patterns. The best PSFs are also continually reinventing their skill sets and ways of working as their client base evolves and they learn new ways of adding client value. The metaphor that suits the PSF is not, in fact, a production line but a fluid, creative network. The most important process is not necessarily the linear movement of work around the organization but the non-linear passage of information and ideas between all areas of

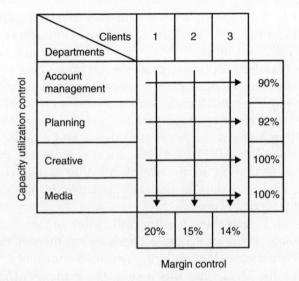

Figure 7.14   *Illustration of matrix management in an efficient PSF*

the firm. A demanding client can be won over at a meeting because of a flash of inspiration from the account handler that might have its origins in a conversation with a different client a day or so before. Structure is not the principle driver of motivation, idea flow or creativity and it is motivation, idea flow and creativity that are the dominant drivers of differentiation.

Despite this, few PSFs push down profit responsibility to the account level. The reason few firms do so is that the management of most PSFs are afraid to empower staff with financial control. Often they will not trust their account managers or senior consultants to set and manage proper budgets. They may even be unwilling to expose the margins achieved on different accounts to the people actually running those accounts under the notion that they might either betray them to the client inadvertently or use the information for competitive purposes should they migrate to another employer. Such neurosis on the part of senior PSF management is surprisingly common, particularly where the FD plays a strong central role. It usually goes hand in hand with suboptimal performance and a skewed client profitability pattern.

The other reason that PSFs often fail to push profit responsibility down to the account level is that they lack the information systems to gather and distribute the information. The IT systems of many PSFs are limited, ledger-based systems that rely on a central accountant inputting professional hours and producing invoices for clients. The systems are not usually designed to help account people establish their own budgets and to monitor costs and revenue performance against a budget. The time of staff data itself is often gathered on paper timesheets and rekeyed centrally. Few PSFs have PC-based timesheeting and few distribute financial information to the desktop either daily, weekly or monthly. Financial data is typically guarded by the CEO and CFO as if it were dangerous.

The result is that there is often little ethic of timekeeping by professionals. Without accurate timekeeping there is no ability to know whether a client is being serviced profitably or incurring overruns. Over time this fosters the typical culture of an underperforming PSF—little regard is given to time; the unique focus of senior people is on keeping the client happy almost irrespective of the resources consumed and the financial performance of the account; rewards are based on client feedback and revenue growth, not margin performance; senior account people develop little skill in budgeting and have little reason to hold themselves to anything but a revenue budget. As a result, there is little knowledge in the system about where resource is being spent or the real level of utilization. As the FD consolidates power, the ethic of central control establishes itself and the process of withholding information hardens. In essence, the firm looks more like a Communist dictatorship than a market system where resource is allocated through market forces on the basis of profit.

The hallmark of most PSFs that have shown consistent high levels of performance is that the people running accounts have profit responsibility and contribute to setting and holding client budgets. They tend to be very conscientious timekeepers. The firm has the ability to desegregate profit information by project and client and distribute this information to the desktop speedily. Management tend to be less concerned about structure and more focused on managing overall capacity combined with healthy positive margins on all client engagements. Rewards are based on profitability as well as revenue growth. The capacity and account contribution picture will look something like the example illustrated in Figure 7.15. This is, needless to say, a rarity. The average sensitivity of PSFs to these issues is low.

Pulling It All Together

In the great race for productivity improvement, PSFs haven't even really left the starting post. But their clients are really beginning to force the pace. This means that they will face tough choices. In the panic for change most PSFs will bolt for structural solutions borrowed from the industrial model. The better ones, however, will focus on the people issues rather than abstract concepts of organization. They will put their energies into devolving responsibility down the organization and harnessing the forces of the internal market to drive resource and time allocation.

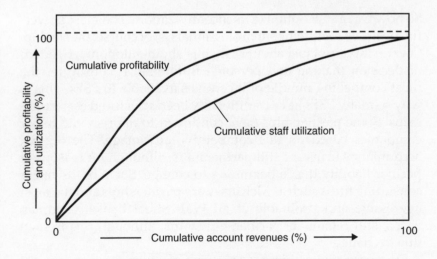

Figure 7.15 *Illustrative optimal account contribution and staff-utilization patterns for a PSF*

RECRUITMENT, INCENTIVES AND
CAREER MANAGEMENT

What drives PSFs are people and what drive people are incentives. The engines of all PSFs are incentives. The interesting thing about incentives is that people are driven not by one thing but by odd clusters of different things. They might range from exposure to senior decision makers, autonomy, office size, titles, to that old staple, cash. In a world economy with an increasing premium on intellectual value-added, the mobility of smart professionals is high and increasing. This means that the degree of sensitivity of individuals to the basket of incentives offered by a PSF tends to be more extreme among PSFs than in a manufacturing firm. The power of the individual "supplier" in the PSF industry is unusually high. This means that a PSF's ability to incentivize its individuals is one of the most important things it has to get right. None of the productivity improvement initiatives we have discussed will yield anything if unaccompanied by well-structured incentives.

The Power of Equity and Partnership

So how can a PSF optimize its incentivization? The most powerful incentive for intelligent professionals is, of course, ownership. Ownership is not just about cash; it is about autonomy, freedom of decision making and personal fulfilment. It constitutes the most compelling bundle of incentives available to PSFs. This is why so many PSFs have traditionally been structured as partnerships. Some partnerships have continued to flourish into major companies based on this competitive advantage. The Big Six accountancy firms are still partnerships, although for reasons of partner liability this is beginning to change. Some of the major consulting firms such as McKinsey are partnerships and the most aggressive and profitable of all Wall Street banks, Goldman Sachs, still retains its partnership status, although this is soon due to change.

Of course, ownership or some form of equity interest does not automatically translate into high earnings growth. The dominant fate of the small privately held PSF is to stay small. The number of partnerships which have achieved critical global mass is gradually being surpassed by the number of global networks which are publically quoted or have been capitalized by financial investors.

The other factor which is overlooked with partnerships is that the motivational benefits of it diminish with size and partner coverage. One highly motivated partner in a firm of ten professionals can have a decisive effect in determining overall performance. Diluted among 200 professionals the impact of that individual will clearly be far less. Many non-equity-holding staff will have their independent client relationships and may not be influenced by the owner's view on how to manage their accounts. The good ones will eventually up and leave if there is no equity tie to the company. The strength of partnerships such as McKinsey is based on the fact that the ratio of partners to staff is quite small (about one in 10–12). Therefore the equity is well diluted among those people who can really make a difference. In some of the Big Six Five accountancy firms where this ratio has grown to 1:20–25 or the investment bonds where it is as high as 1:50, there must ultimately be problems maintaining motivation levels and therefore super-premium quality. The response of Arthur Andersen, for example, has been to begin to promote non-partner track people to levels which equate to that of a partner without the equity status of partnership.

The limiting factor with partnership-driven PSFs is that they are unable to expand at a rate that makes them competitive. By nature they fund themselves through retained earnings since they are not structured to admit external capital. The result is that their ability to acquire other companies, invest in start-up offices or even hire professionals on the speculation that they may bring in business can be somewhat constrained. Their growth is limited to the rate at which they can create new partners and generate retained earnings. In markets where clients are moving fast, and require international servicing capability, this can be a major disadvantage. While there are a handful of successful global partnerships that have taken root over the course of half a century, the outlook for medium-sized or small partnerships is not great given their inability to fund international growth.

The partnership model is an organic growth model. The large

partnerships all have century-long histories. In the race for consolidation and globalization, small and medium-size firms do not have the time to rely on the gradual expansion required before a partnership hits critical mass. Therefore, it is unlikely that the partnership will continue to be the dominant model for the PSF it has been in the past.

Limited Companies

Most PSFs which have reached critical mass tend to have made the transition away from partnerships. They will typically be structured as a limited company and will have admitted external capital to fund growth. They might have a financial investor, have sold out partly to another trade buyer, or have gone public either independently or as part of a larger quoted group. The pattern of transition to institutional ownership as part of the growth process raises the issue of how to replicate the motivational benefits of partnership without distributing too much equity to professionals and diluting shareholdings.

Limited companies have plenty of room for manoeuvre when it comes to creating equity-like incentives. There is a fairly standard hierarchy of methods available to PSFs to simulate ownership rewards. At the bottom end there is the annual bonus, usually paid in cash. This is pretty much standard among all PSFs (both partnerships and limited companies). Bonus plans have the motivational benefit of tying individual performance to firm performance since the bulk of the payments available under most bonus schemes are driven by the volume of operating profit before tax or OPBT generated by the business. In essence they have the same quality as dividends except they are taken out pre-tax with the associated tax shield advantages for the firm. For most firms this also represents an opportunity to shift away from fixed to variable costs, with the benefit of moving risk from the firm to the employee and also lowering the ongoing monthly cash demands of the business and therefore its borrowing needs. Firms can also earn interest on bonus payment accruals or provisions created through the course of the year.

The key with bonus plans is the ability of the firm to correctly differentiate between the relative contribution of employees and to make variable compensation a significant part of overall compensation. The process of performance evaluation has evolved rapidly over the past decade, progressing from standard top-down appraisal forms to the 360° evaluation.[12] The problem PSFs face is that significant bonuses to key professionals can only really be made on the basis of quantifiable economic contribution. Otherwise it is all dependent on the vagaries of personal judgement. Systems such as the 360° evaluation process are attempts to turn personal judgement into an objective system by diluting the impact of one wonky viewpoint. While they can often serve as good means to help professionals learn from each other in a constructive fashion, they are not usually a powerful platform on which to base variable pay, particularly if it is a high percentage of total remuneration.

Most firms which attempt to base bonus systems on subjective peer group measures such as the 360° process, fail to shift a really significant proportion of total compensation from fixed to variable without causing paralysing internal politics. Typically the majority of firms will limit the really significant bonus schemes (say, above 50% of base salary) to the very top tier of management or, more specifically, to those with P&L responsibility which is typically only the MD and the FD of an office.

The reason most firms are stuck with incentive structures which are not based on significant variable earnings is that profit accountability is held by a small number of people. Unless P&L accountability is held at the account level (which is a rarity), it is tough to understand the exact contribution of individuals to firm performance. Firms which bonus heavily as a percentage of base salary tend to be those that make their account people P&L responsible. While it doesn't always hold true, they will also tend to be the most profitable. Good people will get heavily rewarded and bad people will be swiftly dispatched in proportion to their ability to create profit for the company.

---

[12] The 360° evaluation system involves an individual being reviewed and, in turn reviewing, all the key people with whom they work, including their bosses. As such, the evaluation process is two-way and has multiple viewpoints.

Paying Up

The classic form of the annual bonus is cash. The problem with cash is that it is simply handed over and then disappears. Professionals tend to view each payment as the end of a discrete work period and it doesn't necessarily generate a longer-term bond with the company. In other words, cash doesn't have the effect of mirroring equity dividends. More sophisticated PSFs have responded to this by breaking bonuses into two prevalent types short-term incentive plans (STIPs) and long-term incentive plans (LTIPs). STIPs are usually paid at the end of each year in question like any normal bonus, with the difference that they will often be paid partly in share options[13] (or phantom share options[14]). LTIPs, by contrast, will be granted annually but typically will not be paid out for a number of years during which time they will accumulate interest or, in the case of shares, dividends and capital appreciation. Usually they will be paid in shares or options which will further delay pay-out and pin it to future performance. The key issue, of course, is the split between LTIPs and STIPs.

The effect of the delayed cumulative payments is obviously to bind in professionals well beyond the year of the award. They are also more cash efficient for the company. The share or option component simply reinforces this. It is a classical sign of a mature and sophisticated PSF that it awards a high proportion of variable compensation (say, around 50%) in the form of a deferred payment mechanism which is less liquid than cash.

Of course, money is not the only motivator. In fact, as many studies have shown, it can have a corrosive effect on morale if used excessively. The investment banking industry, for example, is notorious for its high bonus levels. It is able to grant them because most of the high earners have direct profit contribution either as individual traders, salespeople or deal makers. However, this has neither resulted in consistent superior margin

---

[13] Share options typically only vest after a set period of time and if the firm performs to certain benchmarks which, in the case of a quoted firm, might relate to growth in EPS or total shareholder returns over the period.

[14] Phantom share options give the right to receive shares but with no underlying option agreement or no underlying security at the time of issue. They might be awarded before a firm floated and only crystallize into proper instruments at that point in time.

performance in the sector nor has it promoted professional loyalty. The volatility of earnings and the rate of employee churn are among the highest for the entire PSF sector. Shareholders are often left with the scraps after the bonus pool is cleared out.

The really good firms find mechanisms to motivate which carry a lower net price tag for the firm than cash or shares and which foster an equally strong commitment on the part of professionals. The most significant of these is training. A cohesive three- to five-year training programme, based partly on practical experience and partly on classroom sessions, can be deployed to the same effect as an options programme—it creates more value for the professional the longer they stay with the firm. It also has the enhanced effect of improving the professional's contribution to the firm and hence could, in principle at least, be self-liquidating. The reality is, however, that most firms don't train; they bonus in cash. Training tends to be viewed by management not as an employee benefit incremental to bonus schemes but as a company expense. As soon as markets toughen such expenses are the first to go. Training is certainly not viewed as a component of the reward system by most PSFs.

The most common method of incentivizing without cash is titular promotion. Most PSFs are riddled with a plethora of titles because titles are "free". The more frequently a firm feels obliged to promote, the more of a pile-up tends to occur at VP (Vice President) level. Most firms succumb to title inflation since it can often be done with little rise in salary. There is, however, a cost. It tends to disrupt the internal professional balance and accelerate churn as expectations of rapid promotion are fostered and disappointed. Like all inflation, it cannot go on indefinitely.

Pulling It All Together

So how do you tell whether a firm is good or bad at motivating employees? The basic key indicators are the rate of employee churn (annual replaced leavers, adjusted for severance and dismissal, as a percentage of total staff) and the ratio of variable pay to fixed pay in the remuneration pot. Clearly, the higher the variable ratio and the lower the churn, the more successful the incentive strategy (Figure 7.16).

The incentive issue is becoming an ever more critical one not only for PSFs but for all companies whose competitive advantage is founded on intellectual capital. As people businesses continue to expand at a faster rate than industry, the competition for a limited pool of talent is accelerating and the non-equity professional is becoming an ever more fickle beast. The rate of inflation in most Western economies is below 5% but the rate of inflation of PSF wages is probably in excess of 10% on average. This means that a PSF's ability to create and manage a compelling incentive scheme is probably the single greatest determinant of its long-term success.

The result is that successful PSFs tend to be excellent managers and incentivizers of employees. Other industrial and service businesses have plenty to learn from the PSF sector. Most Western industry is increasingly dependent on differentiating their products and capturing value-added to remain competitive rather than following a strategy of competing on low costs. This

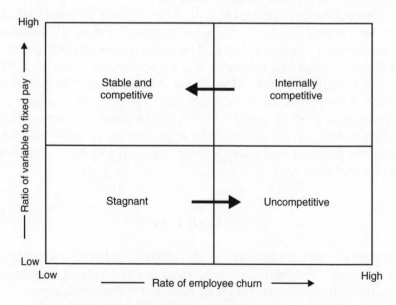

Figure 7.16   *Illustrative relationship between remuneration mix and employee churn*

means that the intellectual capital of their workforce is rapidly becoming more valuable to them than the book value of their fixed asset base. As this trend accelerates, all Western firms are beginning to face the same problem—how to attract and hang onto highly marketable talent.

In the good old days, with factories full of low-skilled manual workers marshalled by unions, firms knew where they stood. With primadonnas and PhDs they are no longer so sure. The classic HR department approach to managing people usually falls flat on its face. Grey, underqualified HR professionals are never good at attracting talent. The only people who can do that are senior managers themselves. It probably makes more sense for industrial firms to use successful PSFs as benchmarks of best practice on incentive issues than firms in their own sector. It is rare indeed that an industrial will have thought as hard about incentives as a successful PSF!

FINANCIAL AND PROCESS CONTROL

The PSF sector has a reputation for lacking the same level of financial control and competence as good industrial firms. There are the old stories of ballooning expense accounts, the escalating salaries, the unjustifiably flash office space and an obsession with fast cars. Large swathes of the PSF industry are dismissed as "life style" businesses by their erstwhile industrial cousins. There is no doubt that this view has influenced the capital markets which regard PSFs as to some extent "flaky" (despite being dominated by PSFs themselves) .

To some degree these attributions are true of the average PSF. In the case of privately held firms where most of the cash is withdrawn as salary and dividends by the owners, the need for rigorous financial controls is often felt unnecessary as long as the business is throwing off adequate cash. The result is that the PSF sector in general tends to attract lower-calibre financial professionals than industrials. This in turn influences the sophistication of their management of the balance sheet as well as the P&L. Few PSFs successfully access the financial markets for either debt or equity but rely on retained earnings to fuel growth.

The issue of control in many PSFs is not limited solely to

management of the balance sheet and P&L. It also extends to the issue of how well the underlying processes of the firm itself are managed. Unsophisticated financial management is an expression of an underlying lack of proper operational control. Finances are usually a symptom, not a cause.

Financial Control

Most PSFs are managed on a standard set of "hygiene factors" which are simpler than their industrial counterparts, namely:

- Gross margin
- Operating margin
- Staff to revenue ratio
- Conversion rates

These measures are different from the usual ones associated with industrials where turnover and capital are always the denominators of key ratios.

As we have already touched on, the difference between turnover and gross margin is critical for most PSFs. In PSFs, turnover tends to include the value of bought-in services which have in fact been performed by other firms but have been bundled in as part of the PSF's deliverable. As such, the PSF has to pay these firms out of their billings to the client. In the case of a full-service advertising firm, for example, turnover or "billings" would include the value of the media space bought on behalf of the client. In a design firm it would include the cost of external print production. In an investment bank it would include the value of securities and debt placed on behalf of a client in the markets.

The gross revenue minus bought-in services is termed gross income or fee income and is the equivalent of revenue in an industrial company. Therefore most PSFs will focus on their gross margin relative to turnover or the revenue yielded on services delivered to the client. Gross margin, expressed as turnover minus the value of bought-in services as a percentage of turnover, is an indicator of the efficiency with which the firm generates income.

The operating margin is measured by dividing operating income by gross income (or gross margin). In an industrial firm most managers focus on pre- and after-tax margins. This is less useful in the case of PSFs. The key item between operating and pre-tax income is the net interest charge or net interest income. In industrials, which usually have debt on the balance sheet, the net interest charge is often a significant number, reflecting the capital intensivity of operations. The ability of the industrial to manage the balance sheet will be as important as its ability to manage the P&L. By contrast, in PSFs the net interest position is often awash. It will generate interest income as a result of managing the balance of payment for bought-in services. Conversely, it will typically have a low debt interest charge. The result is often a small positive net interest income.

As a result, operating income is often the most useful basis for assessment of performance ratios in PSFs. The important thing is that operating margin has to be measured off gross income and not turnover. The mistake of using turnover as a denominator often results in analysts thinking margins are low when in fact they are typically very high in a PSF.

On the cost side, the cost structure of all PSFs (provided they haven't moved into a ludicrously large building) is driven by their staff costs and most FDs will simply monitor their staff cost-to-revenue ratio. The staff cost-to-revenue ratio, gross margin and operating margin are often the only variables by which they will steer the ship. Of course, what this ignores are the underlying drivers of fee capacity and fee conversion as we have already discussed in Chapter 6. Also, relying on staff–cost ratios can be misleading as key professionals with equity stakes will often maximize the amount they draw from the firm pre-tax to minimize the firm's taxable income. We will come onto these distorting effects presently in Chapter 8.

Conversion Rates

Most privately held PSFs tend not to use P&L ratios to measure their rate of improvement over time. They simply look at static ratios on a year-by-year basis. The emphasis tends to be on revenue growth solely. The better firms will focus on conversion rates. Conversion is the efficiency with which incremental revenue can be dropped to the bottom line. It is simply measured by dividing incremental profits by incremental gross margin. With most PSFs the greater their rate of growth, the more profitable they should be as they convert incremental revenue to margin— e.g. adding income faster than they need to add cost. This usually works in a step function as full capacity utilization is reached after a certain amount of additional revenue and then new people have to be hired (Figure 7.17). Whereas industrials typically have to add costs before they can grow revenues, PSFs can win projects and income before they staff-up to fully service the client properly. Efficient PSFs will therefore usually aim for conversion rates in the range of 20–40%, although this number will modulate depending on the available capacity and the timing of the hiring cycle.

The implication of the conversion rate is to suggest that it is easier for a PSF to increase its profitability the faster it is growing revenues. In industrials it is common to find high levels of profitability among firms which are showing low growth. This

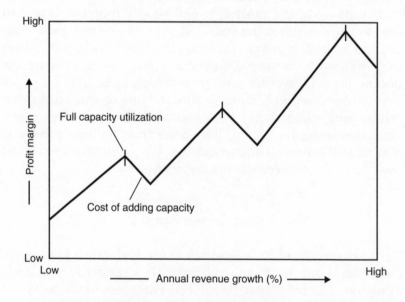

Figure 7.17   *Illustrative relationship between revenue growth and profitability in a typical PSF*

usually occurs because they are harvesting—exploiting a strong historical market position to extract maximum profits while suppressing investment and depreciation. This position cannot be maintained indefinitely of course, but renewed investment to grow the top line will almost certainly lower reported earnings initially. In the world of PSFs things move faster. It is unusual to find a firm that can harvest effectively for more than a couple of years without beginning to lose pitches and professionals and suffer rapid margin erosion. There are a few exceptions in sectors where client assignments last for years without regular review, such as the advertising industry, but this is not the dominant pattern. It is more often the case that a firm showing the highest level of growth will also show the highest margins, unless it is winning business by underpricing, which is not a sustainable strategy among PSFs due to their weak balance sheets.

In general, then, the P&Ls of PSFs are simple, premised on four basic measures. It is, therefore, surprising how variable the results of firms in similar sectors can be. Obviously a lot of this has to do with the quality of client relationships and the client wins during a given year. However, it is equally a reflection of the variable quality of financial control in many of these businesses. The measures used are not sophisticated and do not consider whether returns on shareholder equity (whether in the form of shares or partner time) are being maximized. This brings us back to our economic model illustrated in Figure 4.2 (p. 37). The usual mistake in running a PSF is that there is no understanding of how fee capacity is driven and how it is converted to profit. Hence the volatility in the earnings of many firms.

The Balance Sheet

As we have already discussed, the balance sheet of PSFs looks somewhat different from most industrials. On the assets side they tend to have little in terms of material fixed assets worth mentioning and on the funding side they tend to rely on retained earnings (Figure 7.18). Because owners have often dividended out the after-tax earnings of the firm rather than reinvesting

Assets   Source of funding

・Current assets   ・Current liabilities
 − cash   − trade creditors
 − WIP   − bank overdrafts
 − receivables   − capital leases
                              − taxes due
                              − prepaid expenses

                    70%

                     =

・Fixed assets   ・Long term liabilities
 − tangible assets   10%   − bank debt
  ・building   − preference shares
  ・fixtures and fittings

                              ・Equity
 − intangible assets   − called up and
  ・trademarks   20%   additional paid
  ・goodwill   in capital
                               − revaluation reserve
                               − retained earnings

Figure 7.18   *Illustrative simplified balance sheet of a typical PSF*

them, the balance sheet is usually small relative to the revenues of the firm. The bulk of the balance sheet is tied up with working capital. Since the cash reserves of most PSFs are small and their overdraft facilities tend to be shallow, they are dependent on managing net working capital needs closely to keep solvent.

On the asset side of the net working capital equation, most client receivable terms are around six weeks. Because of the strong negotiating position of larger clients, this inevitably gets stretched. However, the other common reason for stretched terms is internal—the accounts department of the PSF issues an invoice and the Account Director fails to follow up to ensure that the client is fully aware that it is due. Really bad payment terms can regularly extend to four months in many PSFs due to internal laxity. The more sophisticated PSFs find ways to mitigate the impact of payment delay, usually by breaking projects into regular, equal monthly payment schedules with full settlement terms at the end of the year. Alternatively they might segment payments into a regular monthly retainer at cost combined with incremental billing at key points in a project which will deliver the profit.[15]

The sophistication of a firms staging arrangements makes all the difference to their cash performance and the health of their balance sheet. The key is to ensure that regular inflows match regular outflows and that spikes of bought-in costs are matched by quickly paid or preferably pre-paid spikes of income from the client. Figure 7.19 illustrates the client driven cash flow dynamics of most PSFs.

The key to current asset management is that a firm's account professionals take the billing process seriously. They are usually in the best position to call up the client and speed the payment process without causing annoyance since they work with them regularly. A poor firm will be characterized by professionals who are reluctant to call the client on slow payment and are not fully aware of the cash implications of late payment. This will leave the overstretched CFO to make cold calls without understanding the delicacies of the client situation. This can cause real problems.

---

[15] Larger PSFs may even factor out their receivables in order to take the strain off their balance sheet. In such a case, the pre-payment received from the factor should be treated as short-term debt.

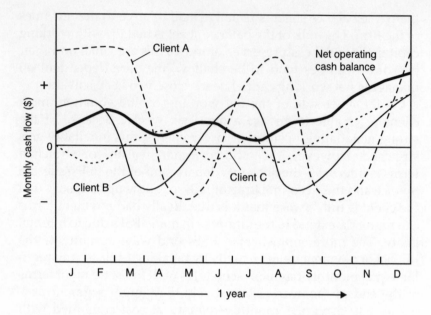

Figure 7.19   *Illustrative cash flow dynamics of a good-performing PSF*

Poor account people will also tend to be bad at differentiating between clients which are systematically good payers and those that are bad, resulting potentially in the firm favouring the latter on the basis of some professional criteria without taking the cash issue into consideration. If the firm gathers a set of clients who are bad payers it will quickly get itself into trouble.

The acid test of a firm's ability to manage receivables is its bad debt ratio, or the proportion of billed work which has to be written off due to non-payment. A good firm will typically keep this between 1–3% and a bad firm will range in normal circumstances between 3–5%. Good PSFs will typically carry about 40–50 days of receivables.[16] Problem firms usually show their colours at around 60–90 days of receivables.[17]

Current assets are composed principally of receivables and

[16] Days receivables is calculated by dividing revenues into receivables and multiplying by 365 days.

[17] In most PSFs there will be banded receivables—0–30 days, 30–60 days and above 90 days. Above 90 days should account for less than 10% of receivables. The period of payment is as important as the ratio of bad debt, since receivables have to be funded.

work in progress or WIP (the equivalent of inventory). Work in progress is an even more incisive indicator than receivables. A firm's ability to control the amount of work it is doing without billing the client offers a great insight into the quality of its internal controls. The classic hallmark of a poorly managed firm is a ballooning WIP number because professionals do not bother to inform the accounts department that a piece of work has been performed and do not view it as important that regular bills get prepared and sent. Firms often lack an ability even to track WIP accurately. The sure sign that this is the case is a large volume of write-offs—that is, the proportion of WIP which does not get converted into receivables on a monthly basis. A good firm will usually stand at 5% or less of write-offs and a bad firm will range in normal circumstances from 5% to 10%. WIP should never exceed receivables and a comfortable ratio is around 50% (assuming billing is monthly). Failure to convert WIP into receivables is cost straight to the bottom line and cash out of the bank!

Sources of Funding

The other side of the equation is predominantly payables. Most PSFs buy in services and then recharge them as part of a client project. These bought-in services will constitute the bulk of the payables pile for most PSFs. Clearly it is in the cash interests of all PSFs that the payment terms for such suppliers should be longer than their own terms for client receivables or else there will be a cash flow problem. However, it is easily abused. The temptation for weaker PSFs with a poor receivables record is to stretch payables out. The problem with this is that after a year or so of slow payments the better suppliers will begin to refuse to work with the PSF and it will be stuck with the duds. This will immediately impact the quality of its work, its ability to retain clients and hence its revenue growth. A firm with a poor receivables record will typically stretch payables and will be on the slippery slope to non-competitiveness.

The second major item is prepaid expenses or deferred income. It is common for PSFs to insist that clients pay them a contribution to their costs upfront as part of a staging arrangement. The higher the prepaid expenses number is as a percentage of WIP (known as net WIP), the better. A high ratio will indicate good cash flow management by the PSF.

The other current liability to keep an eye on is the salary and bonus reserve or accrual. It is the cheapest trick in the book for a PSF to control a poor cash situation by delaying payment of its professionals. It may do this by deferring salary in the promise of a future bonus payment. The impact of deferring salary and then not paying bonuses on the professional quality of the firm going forward is obvious. Deferring payment is, of course, legitimate as long as a reserve is created out of earnings to make this payment. Therefore, accruals for payment can usually be taken as signs of good management.

It is actually more common to find that an earnings enhancement is being achieved artificially by the key partners lowering their own salaries in order to boost reported earnings. In such cases they will usually take out the bulk of free cash in the form of a dividend without knocking their financial ratios. The most common time to find this, of course, is prior to an attempted sale of the company where a multiple will typically be applied to reported after-tax earnings to determine the sale price, as we will explore presently.

Lastly, there is balance sheet debt. Most PSFs will run an overdraft facility which will push up the apparent leverage of the firm at any given point in time. However, it will usually come down to a net zero position over the course of a full year as the client receivables cycle is completed. Some PSFs will also carry bank debt and possibly a bunch of preferred stock if there has been a financial investor which will carry a coupon.[18] Up to a point, bank debt is a good thing since it boosts the returns to equity holders because of the tax shield effect of interest[19] as well as by supporting a higher volume of revenue per share. Preferred

---

[18] Venture capitalists and other financial investors typically invest in preferred stock because it has a secure cash flow from the dividends but can usually be converted into ordinary stock in the event that the company is sold, so that they can benefit from any capital appreciation. Preferred stock also ranks above ordinary stock in the event of a liquidation in terms of its claim on assets in any disposal and hence is less risky.

[19] Interest is tax deductible and therefore creates a shield against tax which is worth the interest multiplied by the tax rate in terms of cash to shareholders. Debt is therefore an efficient way to enhance returns to shareholders as long as the firm can afford the interest payments.

stock does not have this cash flow benefit, although, since cou-
pons are paid after tax, they do not hit the P&L above the PBT
line.

The more common situation among PSFs is a lack of leverage
and therefore lower rates of ROE than would normally be expected from a comparably sized industrial firm with normal
levels of debt.[20] One reason for wariness about debt by PSF
management is the correct assumption that the debt carrying
capacity of most PSFs is lower than their industrial counterparts. A banker might well feel happy with an interest coverage ratio of four to six times for an industrial.[21] For its PSF
counterpart, a banker might feel uncomfortable with it drop-
ping below eight times. The reason is simple—the volatility of
earnings is seen to be potentially higher if the firm is not well
run.

Off-balance-sheet Items

Of course, what does not appear on the balance sheet is more
important than what does. This is far truer for PSFs than for
industrials. The two key off-balance-sheet liabilities are rental
obligations for office space and operating leases for office equipment. The annual rent is usually the second biggest item in the
cost structure of a PSF. It is a common temptation in an upswing
for PSFs to take on a greater property commitment than the
business can comfortably handle in a downswing. This mistake
has been repeated time and again. Long, non-break lease clauses
and irregular rent reviews should raise the blood pressure if they
are combined with a high building cost-to-revenue ratio in excess
of 12%. Good PSFs will view lease obligation as a form of debt,
providing the firm with leverage to increase its market profile
and professional appeal. Therefore, as with any form of debt, an

---

[20] ROE can be calculated using the Du Pont formula:

$$\frac{\text{Profits}}{\text{Equity}} = \frac{\text{Profits}}{\text{Sales}} \times \frac{\text{Sales}}{\text{Assets}} \times \frac{\text{Assets}}{\text{Equity}}$$

As this formula shows, the level of leverage in the firm, or assets over equity, directly
drives return on equity because it allows a higher volume of business to be financed
for the same amount of equity investment in the business. The constraining factor is
that the firm has got to be able to meet the interest payment obligations of the debt.

[21] Interest coverage is measured by dividing operating profit by interest expense.

operating income (less lease costs) coverage ratio of all debt interest plus annual property costs of in excess of three times is sensible.

The property issue has historically been contentious. Most PSFs based much of their client and professional allure on the position and originality of their office space. Hence there is a strong argument for leveraging up the balance sheet in terms of property commitments. However, this argument is becoming increasingly less valid. Most PSFs conduct much of their business at the client site and as a result the standard office utilization is between 20% and 30% at any point in time. The fact that the client and employees are usually not present also militates against the location argument. With the advent of e-mail and PC videoconferencing, this trend is simply being reinforced.

As we will come onto, the volume of space can also usually be radically reduced to accommodate peak demand through the use of "hotelling" and "hot-desking". Arthur Andersen, for example, is reputed to have reduced its office space per professional from around 120 ft^2 to around 60 ft^2 by taking away individual desks and moving to a rent-a-desk format. The *quid pro quo* is usually an offsetting weight of investment in the IT necessary to support remote communications, e-mail and an Intranet. This is, however, almost certainly a more productive use of money than sinking it into property.

In terms of other off-balance-sheet items, operating lease commitments for capital items such as photocopiers and computer systems will usually hover around 1–3% of revenues. Once they begin to exceed 5%, again, the blood pressure should increase. However, the really important off-balance-sheet items of any PSF are, of course, the talent, skills, brand reputation and client franchise of the firm. Sometimes these will be embodied in a goodwill[22] number if the firm has been assembled through acquisitions. But, more often than not, this value will not appear on the balance sheet at all. This means that the net asset value of any PSF is no guide whatsoever as to the value of the firm. It

---

[22] Goodwill is the difference between the book value of a firm and the price another firm pays to acquire it. In essence it represents the difference between the book value and the market value of a firm but will only appear in the balance sheet if an acquisition has occurred.

would not be atypical for an acquisition price to be in excess of twenty times net asset or book value.[23] The balance sheet is a useful indicator of the cash management abilities of a PSF and its liquidity. It is not, however, any guide to underlying asset value.

Cost management

Most PSFs are top-line rather than cost focused. They tend to add cost in expectation of revenue rather than removing cost to enhance profit. The focus is always on turnover growth. The reason is simple—client acquisition is what drives most PSF professionals emotionally. It is sexy, fun and high-profile. Financial controllers are left in the wake of primadonna rain-makers to worry about maintaining margins. This means in most PSFs there is ample room to enhance margin performance if the will is there on the part of management.

As we have already discussed, the key cost is people and, in most PSFs, this cost is effectively fixed. The decision to fire people on the basis of reduced workload is correctly viewed as highly damaging to long-term performance. It is far easier to swallow temporarily low margins and go looking for new client revenue than risk shattering delicate professional confidence. The problem for most PSFs is the cyclicality of workload which, if they gear up to accommodate the peaks, means they will be over capacity for a significant proportion of the year. Effectively they can have a fixed cost base in a highly variable revenue cycle.

The answer, of course, is to turn as much of that fixed cost base variable. The first way to do this is to focus on freelancing as opposed to permanent employment. Freelancers tend to be pervasive in most PSF sectors, often as a result of being laid off by larger firms or even clients. Their hourly cost tends to be higher than their full-time counterparts but they are a variable cost and can be deployed only when the project margin justifies it. Some of the more adventurous PSFs will double their capacity with the use of freelancers and fundamentally shift the basis of their cost

[23] Book value is simply the value of the firm's current, fixed and intangible assets less all liabilities.

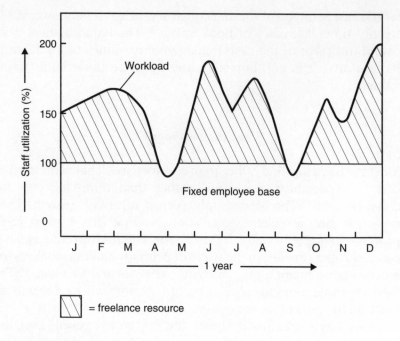

Figure 7.20   *Illustrative capacity utilization for a PSF making structural use of freelance resource*

structure in line with demand (Figure 7.20). In essence this means that they can "chase demand".[24]

The majority of PSFs, however, will not use freelancing as a structural solution but only as an occasional remedy. The reason is simple—there is a natural tendency to distrust the quality of outside people, and a discomfort with letting non-employees get too close to their clients. They will also often fail to understand the margin improvement and risk reduction opportunity that comes from matching the nature of the cost base to that of the revenue cycle.

Despite the fact that PSFs rarely use it structurally, freelancing is the future model of the PSF. The brand of the established firm will remain an important guarantee of quality for the client. Established firms will also be the only way a client can get

[24] Chasing demand means shifting capacity as client revenues are won. Few industrials can do this; instead they have to forecast demand out for a period and add capacity in expectation of hitting the forecast.

large-scale servicing and access to coordinated global coverage. Therefore, freelancers and independents will remain limited in the type of work they can source directly from a client base— there is little chance of freelancers gaining market share from established PSF brands (the direct market penetration of freelancers in a PSF sector such as marketing communications stands at about 5%). However, PSF brands themselves will move from being large permanent employers of full-time staff to being hubs for a large volume of freelance talent built around a core of full-time senior professionals. It is likely that freelancers will primarily plug the gap most PSFs have among middle-ranking professionals, performing a lead role in the execution of assignments but not leading the client relationship.

For the PSF this will obviously provide the benefit of steering away from the endemic capacity management problems they face. It will also give them the benefit of a set of professionals who are highly personally committed to their trade, who are acutely aware of their hourly billing rates and the number of hours they consume on each task. They will tend to be better at managing their time than full-time employees and may even be more experienced since they will have seen a wide number of client and PSF environments. They may even be more talented since creatively talented people seem often to find it tough to stomach nine-to-five full-time employment.

As we have already discussed, the second way of shifting the cost structure from a fixed to a variable basis is to change professional remuneration to a performance-based system. The average PSF will have a fixed to variable ratio of remuneration of around 70/30. In fact, the target should be nearer 50/50. That difference of 30% represents value most PSFs have left on the table, particularly if the variable component were to be linked to margin performance as well as top-line growth.

Non-professional Staff Costs

The staff cost number is often assumed to contain nothing but professional cost. Of course, life is never that simple. There are the secretaries, accountants, building maintenance staff, computer people, etc. Firms rarely compare the ratio of non-client billing people to billable professionals. Yet usually back-office staff will constitute as much as 20% of total staff costs. Typically, there will be as many as one secretary for every three professionals. Once established, back-office employee costs are effectively a fixed cost, further raising the bar of the volume of business the firm needs to generate in order to break even. Typically, firms will be quicker to fire junior professionals in periods of downturn than to reduce this fixed-cost burden which adds far less client value. The point about this cost pile is that, since it adds no direct client value, it does not significantly help to differentiate the firm.

There are many things a PSF can do to both reduce back-office staff costs and to turn these cost items variable. The role of the secretary as typist and message taker can be effectively eliminated through the use of PCs, local networks and voice mail. There is little justification in most situations for more than one secretary for five or more professionals. It is usually far better for a PSF to hire junior account staff who can do some of the menial work but effectively bill it out to the client rather than constitute overhead. Areas of back-office functions such as building maintenance and computer repair can be subcontracted. Lawyers and accountants can be used on an hourly basis. Through these methods, the good PSF will get the indirect staff cost number down to around 10–15% of total staff costs at a maximum and turn up to 50% of it variable.

Rechargeables

The other item related to direct costs that often gets little attention is rechargeables. Professional expenses such as travel, entertainment and other out-of-pocket costs (sometimes referred to as OOPs!) usually account for up to 20% of professional fees billed to the client. In consulting they might get as high as 40% and in advertising they will typically be much lower at around 10%. Usually the PSF will have agreed with each client a threshold for rechargeable expenses. The problem comes when this has been exceeded. Uncharged expenses fall straight against the bottom line. A high percentage of uncharged expenses will be a sure sign of a poor time-management process and little attempt to track profitability by client. Like WIP for an industrial, it is a classic symptom of bad underlying management.

Office Space

As we have already discussed, the second biggest item in the cost structure of PSFs is the cost of the building. In most PSFs the building is viewed as an important driver of revenue growth. Clients get turned on by a good building and good professionals want to work in one. The result is that building costs are often as high as 15% of revenue. The other result is that many PSFs, particularly those within the second and third stages of the PSF life cycle,[25] tend to overrent. The problem with the space bill is that it is a fixed cost in an industry with both seasonal and long-term cyclicality. It is a common mistake for a growing PSF to commit to a major building in expectation of growth and then find its ability to invest in the people necessary to capture and service new revenue strangled by its property costs. This then becomes a very hard downward spiral to reverse.

The cost of a building has two dimensions—cost per square foot and square feet per professional. The cost per square foot is largely driven by location rather than office quality. Location is, of course, important to PSFs. All the investment banking activity in New York is focused on Wall Street. A lot of the advertising and production activity in London centres around Soho. The global consulting industry is centred on Cambridge, Massachusetts. Software support is focused around San Francisco. This clustering of PSFs serves the role of a marketplace for clients, professionals and suppliers. If your stall is in the suburbs who is going to find you? Landlords are not blind to this phenomenon and rents around PSF cluster areas tend to be steep since properties are in effect creating equity for the PSFs present there.

Square feet per professional is driven by the efficiency of space usage. There have always been standard industry practices dictating the space fundamentals. Partners and VPs get offices, the rest are herded about. Each employee gets enough space to

---

[25] Refer back to Chapter 2.

accommodate a fixed desk, filing and other creature comforts. Physical positions tend to be personalized and denote professional standing. Typically, departments will be grouped by floor or, if the firm is located on a single floor plate, they will be separated by walls. The resulting layout will be an odd mixture of offices and open spaces, with functional groups separated by walls and corridors. The analyst trying to understand the flow of work through the organization will usually be completely bemused.

The gravitation towards such industry norms is reinforced by professionals moving regularly between firms. This collectively has the effect of dictating the approximate square footage deemed acceptable based on former experience. The result is a normalization of between 100 and 150 ft^2 per professional, enough room to swing lots of cats!

Over the last five years things have begun to change dramatically. The historical drivers of location are rapidly falling away. As communications links such as e-mail, fax and videoconferencing have made real-time data communications a possibility, the need to maintain an expensive office presence in the "hot districts" has lessened (although not disappeared). Client organizations have also grown more sensitive to the fact that fees include a hefty overhead charge and, since they are rarely located in the hot districts themselves, have grown resentful at the idea that they are subsidizing the life style of their flash PSF suppliers. The more competitive PSFs themselves have also grown more acute to the fact that they can gain advantage from junior professionals spending more of their time working at the client site in borrowed offices and ingraining themselves in the client organization.

The net effect is that most PSFs are able to stretch the boundaries of where they can viably locate. And the advantages of doing so can be great. A building costing $40 per square foot in an unfashionable part of town versus $80 in the hot district will release a lot of cash for internal refurbishment. A bold, innovative interior in a marginal district can send more powerful signals internally and externally than naff space in a hot part of town.

In terms of square footage per employee, the standard assumptions about space needs have also moved on. The first bastion under attack has been the private office. Among more enlightened firms partners are increasingly expected to share open-plan environments with professionals. Open-plan structures make communication flow faster and accountability for productivity far greater—handing work down the hierarchy becomes less viable in open-plan spaces. Along with the disappearance of offices, the walls have begun to come down between departments. Functional groups tend increasingly to be positioned near each other in order to facilitate efficient collaboration on client work. In the most extreme cases department groupings have been disbanded altogether and professionals intermingled on single floor plates to enhance the efficiency of the underlying process.

The more enlightened firms have moved out of vertical buildings with multiple floors and complex corridors which typify central city buildings and shifted to property with single floor plates where interaction is far more efficient. This might be converted former factory space. Medium-sized PSFs moving from individual office lay-outs on multiple floors to open-plan spaces on a single floor plate can achieve significant increases in productivity[26] in addition to savings on real estate costs which can be ploughed back into refurbishment.

The most innovative players have taken this process a stage further. They have geared the capacity of their office space to accommodate the cyclical patterns of professional occupancy. In most PSFs the average utilization of office space is only between 20% and 30% at any one point in time. Clearly it can peak but the pattern will center under 40% in most PSFs as people are at client meetings and travelling (Figure 7.21). Most PSFs are therefore in a position to reduce their volume of space by at least a third without creating undue bottlenecks. Of course, the only way to achieve this is if professionals do not have fixed desks. This is euphemistically called "hot-desking" or "hotelling". Each professional has a "pedestal" for their files and "books" into a desk before coming to the office. Communications and information access is facilitated through Notes or other groupware and all files are stored electronically. Probably the best-known exponent of the virtual office is Arthur Andersen.

---

[26] Productivity is best measured as the dollar volume of revenues per professional.

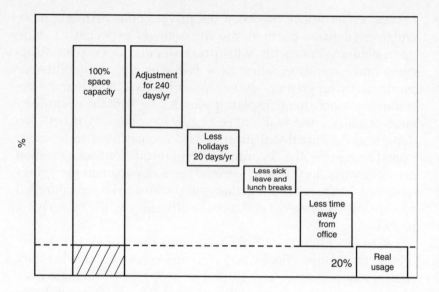

Figure 7.21   *Illustrative typical utilization of office capacity in a PSF*

In general, a real estate cost in excess of 12% of revenue should be regarded with suspicion. It is likely that the firm has over-rented and will have to drive down capex and direct employee costs to rebalance its cost base. It also probably means that it is using very traditional organizational models, has committed little thought to the issue of process flows and has not explored options for productivity improvement. Interestingly, firms which are not imaginative in these areas tend also to be those which are losing their edge. After all, they are meant to be advising clients in one way or another about how they could improve their own business activities. A bad, overrented building is a good litmus test of the business fundamentals of a PSF.

Other Costs

In most PSFs, once you get below staff, OOPs and property costs the rest is something of a murky blur. There are back-room costs such as financial control, accounting, building maintenance as well as a plethora of activities to support the client-facing structure. Much of this cost tends to be semi-fixed such as equipment leases and amortization of office-related expenses. But because it is composed of a collection of individually small items, each of which are dull and do not directly influence the client relationship, they are often ignored. Each small piece tends to fall under the remit of a different manager and ultimate responsibility is often lost in the shuffle. As a result, they have an unpleasant habit of creeping as high as 10% of revenue in the less competitive firm. Again, it is the firm's management of the small things which reveals so much about their management of the overall business!

Pulling It All Together

The cost management capability of a firm clearly influences its ability to drop profit to the bottom line and convert revenue into free cash flow. It is not something for which PSFs in general have a good reputation. It therefore has to be mastered by any PSF wishing to win over sceptical financial investors.

Having said that, PSFs that pursue an increase in profits per partner or per share purely through cost control are doomed. Intrinsic to the ability of PSFs to raise earnings is revenue growth. Without new projects the firm will find it impossible to sustain its reputation and retain good professionals. It will also tend to be stuck with static or declining margins. In most PSFs the fundamental margin would appear to be constrained by the absolute possible ratio of partners to employees. This is not quite true, particularly with globalizing client relationships which can be fostered from a single-partner relationship. In general, margins, as well as absolute profits, will increase as a coefficient of revenue growth.

Basis of control

Financial numbers are only a symptom, not the drivers of performance. What they do allow a firm to do is understand and therefore control their underlying work processes. Using these numbers to control the business is dependent on the right people receiving them on a timely basis and making use of them to condition what they are doing. Even in firms which have invested in the IT to support real-time financial reporting, often the information is not put to use to alter behaviour. And behaviour is what counts in PSFs.

The most common problem with the use (or lack of use) of financial information in PSFs is that the numbers are only looked at in aggregate at the end of each quarter, usually only by the FD and MD. Most firms only produce print-offs of their P&L and the position of receivables and WIP at the office level, aggregated across all accounts. This enables the FDs to understand whether the firm in total is making the money it should be and whether it is billing and collecting as swiftly as it should be doing. If the results are poor the FD will typically first hone in on the issue of the overhead charge and decide whether there is an accumulation of unbilled time (which will get lumped in with general overhead as we will come onto) or an increase in other office costs that can be reversed. He will then turn to the staff–revenue ratio and decide where it could be shaved. He may also turn to the largest accounts and insist that the professionals running them boost revenue growth by pressing the client for new projects.

What he will not be able to do is ensure that, at the level of each account or project, proper margins are being budgeted for and hit or even exceeded. His ability to influence the quality of financial management at the individual account level will be limited for the simple reason that they typically won't have good numbers at the client level. He will also not understand the client situation and will not have credibility with the client to drive alterations in working arrangements. In essence, the firm will be limited to macro-management of a micro-environment.

While only the FD and MD can affect changes in certain variables such as general overhead and overall professional capacity (in cooperation with department heads), it is the account heads who are in a better position to influence the P&L outcome on their individual pieces of business. PSFs are no more really than the aggregate sum of their client accounts. Clearly, if each account is run to a decent target direct margin then the overall outcome for the firm will be positive. At the account level, financial performance will be influenced by the account manager's ability to keep the client happy with the level of servicing while preserving an acceptable staff–revenue ratio. This can only be done by working closely and patiently with the client organization on a day-to-day basis. It cannot be achieved by a mandate from the FD, unless the firm is happy to risk losing the client. But it also cannot be done in the absence of regular data.

Account-based P&L management can lead to substantial margin improvement in most PSFs where it is currently absent. It is, however, unusual to see it carried through rigorously. One reason is that such a system relies on high-calibre, well-trained account staff motivated by the profitability of their accounts. In fact, this is not usually what motivates them at all. It is a natural temptation for any account person to overservice the client since the worst thing that can happen to them is that they lose the client. Losing a major client will usually mean that they lose their job with it. By contrast, little punitive treatment tends to follow systematic overservicing. The client may provide feedback saying he or she is quite happy, new assignments may flow and it will be tough for management to clamp down even if client margins are poor (should they even have the ability to measure them in the first place!). The overservicing cycle is endemic among PSFs.

The interesting thing about overservicing is that it is almost always counterproductive. As soon as the PSF is forced to reign back expenditure when the account goes into loss, the client will usually scream and find another supplier. This will almost certainly mean that the lifetime value[27] of that client relationship has been negative. By contrast, ensuring that the resourcing of the account leaves it highly profitable will often put the PSF in a stronger position. It will be able to invest in the training of its professionals and IT. This will enable it to maintain highly competitive standards that will make it tough for the client to find better servicing.

The key to initiating this virtuous cycle is that the firm understands the need to run a sound P&L on each account and project. This forces account people to take responsibility for managing the underlying process. And it is the process that drives the economics of all PSFs.

---

[27] Lifetime value means the cumulative value of an account over its lifetime with the PSF.

Process control

As we have already touched on, across the whole of the PSF industry there is a complete absence of the rigour of process quality control found in industry. Accordingly, the level of productivity improvements among PSFs over the past decade lags that of industrials despite the impact of information technology. The level of financial control among PSFs, which has improved greatly over the last few years, has not led to its natural extrapolation—a concern with optimizing the underlying process drivers of profitability.

The key to the process of any PSF is time. The question is, does the PSF measure and place absolute value on its only perishable commodity, time? In a typical PSF there are mixed emotions surrounding the time issue. Most professionals will have to fill in timesheets but they will do so as a matter of irksome obligation rather than with an appreciation of how it drives the competitiveness of the firm. Often they will only fill them out once a week, in hardcopy, based on a misty recollection of what happened over the past five days. The sheets will then be dispatched to the accounts department and forgotten about by the professional. Typically, a lot of professional time will be put down as non-client time or lost in the system entirely.

This produces a number of problems. First, it will result in a large pile of unallocated professional time which is not generating fees. This poses the FD with the challenge of deciding whether the firm is over capacity and should fire some people or whether people are just bad timekeepers. Since the pile will tend to be an aggregate of small fractions of everybody's time simple judgements are usually impossible. The result is that this block of time, and therefore direct cost, usually gets assigned as general overhead and redistributed across client accounts as an overhead charge.

Of course, the basis of the reallocation of this overhead is usually the direct reported staff costs on those accounts. This means that error compounds error and the accounts which reported direct staff time accurately tend to get disproportionately hit by an overhead charge. It also means that the final fully loaded cost information by account may bear little relation to reality. In the case of a bad firm, the unallocated professional time pile can exceed 40% of the total capacity in the firm.

Second, as a result of unclear performance numbers by account, it is usually hard for the firm to understand which of its account professionals are doing an outstanding job on a margin basis. This makes it tough to calibrate rewards correctly. Instead of using profitability, they will allocate variable compensation rewards based on revenue growth which is a clean number. Of course, this simply has the effect of compounding the counter-productive behaviour patterns that helped produce the problem in the first place. Professionals will go for revenue growth irrespective of cost and forget about recording time.

As already discussed, there are many natural barriers to getting professionals to take time seriously and to using information on time consumption to condition the overall process. If the job can only make profit with 50 hours of billed time, a professional will typically yield without much of a fight for demands from the client that 100 hours are needed. Of course, he usually fails to persuade the client to pay more. As that behaviour pattern gets reinforced, any concern they might have had with recording time tends to fall away completely (indeed, they usually try to disguise the unbilled time they have spent on the client rather than be forced to confront the client on the issue). Over time the entire office will tend to follow suit and you wind up with a situation where the office is run as a single cost pool. Any adjustments to the cost base are made on the basis of shifting the overall staff–revenue ratio for the office, which is the equivalent of closing the manufacturing line because of a glitch on one particular machine. It costs lots of money in terms of morale and bad decisions.

The better PSFs have ensured that this doesn't happen by making sure that time is valued by its professionals and that the process of capturing time is made easy. The way they usually make people value time is to run P&Ls by job and by client. Each professional establishes a budget on their account with a direct margin target.[28] They are given regular status reports on their performance to budget, and when they begin to approach a potential "overrun" situation they either have to negotiate with the client for more cash or reduced scoping or reduce their

---

[28] The direct margin is revenue less direct costs as a percentage of revenue.

commitment of resource surreptitiously. Typically, variable compensation will be heavily geared to reflect performance to budget in addition to the usual revenue growth measure that drives most PSF compensation schemes. This creates some healthy tension in the system—account leaders will have a vested interest in ensuring that time is recorded accurately by their immediate reports and in avoiding overruns. In essence, it creates internal demand for process control instead of relying on top-down orders from the CEO.

Making the process of measuring time easier, of course, helps the situation. In the best firms timesheeting will be electronic and PCs will be automatically locked in the morning until time-sheets are completed and dispatched. This avoids the usual lag of timesheets being completed only once a week, compounded by the central inputting of data and the manual distribution of results (which usually never happens). In some markets, such as the USA, there are legal problems with imposing penalties for timesheet absenteeism so there are limits to the punitive incentives that firms can employ.

Standard Time

The other twist of sophistication some firms have begun to institute is the use of standard time instead of actual time. The problem with work flow in many PSFs is that it is highly fragmented and, in many aspects, intangible. When is a creative working? When does a consultant come up with the breakthrough idea? Is the banker mulling the deal through in the bath adding client value, indeed more client value than when she is sitting at her desk in the office reading the *Wall Street Journal*? With the growth in home working and international travel this blurring of the value-adding process is increasing dramatically. This leaves the professional with the tough task of determining when they have been working billable time and when they have not. Often the professional is simply unable to make more than an educated guess. The result can often be time lost in the shuffle and the accumulating overhead phenomenon we have already explored.

One answer is to define the separate tasks that have to be

performed to deliver a client product and then attribute standard times to each task. It is always possible to separate out the finite actions that are typically performed as part of a client assignment, using the same methodology as we used in creating a process chart (Figure 7.9). Standard times can be calculated by literally measuring the time taken to perform key tasks and then honing down this average number through experimentation. The first six months of implementing a standard costing system are spent cutting the standard times to reduce any major discrepancy. Professionals then simply tick or click against the box of the appropriate activity once it is completed and timesheets are compiled automatically and the client billed accordingly. The aggregate hours computed through this standard time approach to all accounts held by a firm should, of course, equal the target utilization rate of the firm.

Few firms attempt to implement standard time systems. In essence they are similar to the statistical process control systems[29] employed in manufacturing which allow a firm to understand where process errors are occurring by continually sampling for deviations from the mean. The fact that such systems are rarely explored by PSFs is testimony to their lack of focus on process management and productivity issues and not to the efficacy of the system itself.

Process Measurement

So what are the key measures by which a firm can control its underlying processes? The key measure used in most manufacturing settings is the cycle time or the lapse of time between one finished piece falling off the manufacturing line and the next. The cycle time determines the capacity of the system.[30] In a PSF setting the same logic does not hold. The process is not typically sequential as in a manufacturing line and one project may be

---

[29] Statistical process control systems in manufacturing are based on attributing standard performance criteria to different parts of the process, whether in the form of the time necessary to produce a finished piece or the scrap rates of that part of the process. Once standards are established, performance can be measured by the level of deviation from that standard.

[30] The daily capacity of any production system is measured by dividing the number of minutes the system is running daily by its average cycle time.

temporarily dropped and another picked up as the team continually switches priorities and manages deployment flexibly
against tasks. What matters is how long in total it takes a project
to be completed, both in the sense of the amount of direct professional hours absorbed and the calendar days necessary to complete it. This is called "throughput time". Throughput time is
measured in terms of both professional hours (both billed and
unbilled) and of days elapsed.

Clearly, all projects will have different internal throughput
time targets and also expectations from the client. The key for the
PSF is that, assuming the calendar time is a fixed deadline, the
calendar time and absorbed time don't get out of sync (Figure
7.22). This typically occurs because of poor scheduling and project planning which results in large amounts of time being exp-
ended near the end of a project in order to complete it on time.

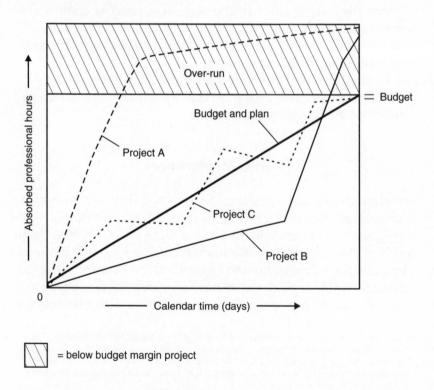

Figure 7.22   *Illustrative dynamics of throughput time in a typical PSF*

Typically, the longer the target calendar time, the more susceptible the process will be to getting out of sync, resulting in overruns.

This occurs for the obvious reason that it is tough to project plan over long periods of time in a highly fluid environment where pitches are being won and lost continually. It also occurs because the longer the time horizon, the less disciplined the client is likely to become in managing its own demands on the PSF. In many respects the length of a project behaves like a financial instrument. The longer the maturity, the more risky it becomes because of likely volatility. This means that most PSFs should raise the overall fee for long projects in anticipation that the scope of work will grow over the period.

As we have already touched on, the second key indicator of process is the overrun. An overrun is the quantity of professional time (with its corresponding cost in terms of salary and overhead allocation) which is in excess of either the budget set for the project or for the time billable to the client (depending on the pricing methodology). Overruns eat straight into the bottom line since they cannot be recharged to any client. They therefore spell financial death for PSFs.

Overruns are typically controlled to below 5% in an efficient PSF. Firms with large overruns usually have poor time management systems and do not measure profitability effectively by project or by client. Overruns have their counterpart in an industrial setting—scrap rates.[31] The interesting distinction between PSFs and industrials is that most industrials are focused like hawks on the volume of scrap they generate and have dedicated tremendous resource to tackling this issue. By contrast, many PSFs do not even know the term "overrun" and certainly rarely focus on it as a determinant of competitiveness. They simply take the hit, subsidizing the client organization with free work.

The close associate of the overrun is utilization. A firm which is suffering high overruns will typically be operating at misleadingly high rates of utilization. Professionals will be inputting heavy time loads against a client, reflecting excessive servicing, and naturally some of this will not be chargeable. Often this

[31] The scrap rate is the percentage of overall production volume that has to be discarded because of irreversible errors.

won't get noticed until, towards the end of a project, the client refuses to pay further yet insists on completion of the project. Alternatively, professionals may be working 20-hour days but logging lots of time as non-billable, sending a completely confusing signal to management.

The dynamic relationship between utilization and overruns is illustrated in Figure 7.23. Utilization is not a positive indicator unless it is combined with low overruns. The combined indicator is "billability" or the percentage of billable hours that are billed to the client. Provided that the economics of a PSF are designed correctly (in terms of professional structure, billing rates and utilization targets), the level of billability of the firm can be aimed at 100% of fee capacity, although the firm will certainly fall short due to overruns and modulations in workload during the course of any period.

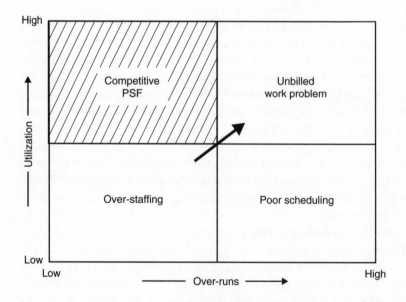

Figure 7.23 *Illustrative relationship between overruns and staff utilization in a typical PSF*

Scheduling and Capacity Planning

Time information is only really useful if it is used to influence the ongoing deployment of professional staff. Most commonly, however, it is only used to bill the client. It will also be used periodically to determine whether there is overcapacity at the office level. However, it is surprisingly uncommon for PSFs to use time data to manage the deployment of their only real asset on an ongoing basis—people. All PSFs have to be reasonable at capacity management and scheduling, otherwise they will quickly go out of business. But typically they do it on the basis of skill and judgement, not systems. This usually means that they are not optimizing the use of their resource.

The problems occur when there are large and volatile projects in play, each of which has some flexibility from the client in terms of commencement and completion. How does the MD work out who should be doing what and when? Sometimes there is a relatively simple solution—charge the client a fixed annual retainer and dedicate staff to the account. This fixes the revenue and the cost but avoids the need to specify individual project schedules. This is effectively how small PSFs with one or two clients operate. Life is easy (but vulnerable!). It is the allure of this simplicity which tempts many PSFs into restructuring into dedicated client teams.

As we already discussed in Chapter 5, there are great advantages to be gained from the flexibility of non-client dedication of staff. The problem is it has to be managed. The poor PSFs avoid the issue of allocating resource by maintaining a level of employees (and hence capacity) which will accommodate the peaks in demand in the system. This means utilization will sometimes be abysmal and overall margins will not be great but the management challenge will be correspondingly low. The good firms have learnt something from the manufacturing world—they will try to chase demand through capacity planning.

The manufacturing world has refined this process of capacity planning to a highly sophisticated degree, beyond the wildest dreams of most PSFs. Many firms habitually use linear programming techniques to achieve optimization. Many PSFs crude models in Excel for resource allocation management. Of course, the problem for PSFs is the need to match up the personality, client fit, skills and charge-out rates of a professional with a client situation. This is at the core of the concept of PSF customization. This means that allocation criteria are beyond those capturable in a linear model.

Scheduling is the last link in the chain of PSF financial management; it is the process which brings a utilization plan to life. All too often it is left up to intuition and feel. If PSF management is prepared to push down profit responsibility to account people, it also has to provide the resource planning tools necessary for them to construct and manage budgets. The most powerful combination in any PSF is a system of account-based P&Ls and sophisticated capacity planning approaches managed by department heads. This combination produces a virtuous matrix of control (refer back to Figure 7.14). The account heads set a budget on each account and project against margin targets and the department heads allocate resource in such a way as to maximize capacity utilization for their department. The result is super-margins. Unfortunately, it is rarely done!

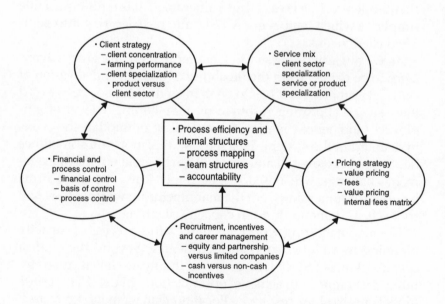

Figure 7.24 *The generic Professional Service Model*

PULLING IT ALL TOGETHER

Whatever the overall attractiveness of any PSF segment, a competitive firm will be able to achieve excellent returns as long as it positions itself correctly. The Professional Service Model is a simple summary of the key levers available to any PSF to achieve a good competitive position in its chosen segments. Typically, different PSFs will focus on one or two levers and forget the rest. It is not uncommon to find people businesses refining their client strategy to a piece of artwork and then going into a spiral of underperformance due to a lack of internal margin controls. To be effective, the six constituents of the PSM have to be internally consistent (Figure 7.24). That means a PSF has to coordinate its hiring and retention of people with its targeting of a client base. It also has to ensure that its pricing strategy takes account of its ability to control costs at an account level and thereby manage its margins tightly. PSFs that underperform or encounter financial constraints almost always do so because they have not taken a balanced approach to managing all the drivers of performance.

8
Corporate Finance and Valuation of PSFs

As we have discussed, the right-hand side of the balance sheet of most PSFs is relatively simple; a small amount of bank debt, usually in the form of an overdraft, a set of current liabilities and a certain amount of retained earnings. In short, PSFs tend to be undercapitalized. They also tend to be financially unsophisticated in terms of their treasury function. This means that the potential returns to shareholders are not maximized through balance sheet structure, the cost of debt is not efficient and both the growth prospects and the market value prospects of the firm are constrained.

The usual assumption is that private PSFs are too exposed to debt. In fact quite the opposite is usually the case. They tend to be systematically underleveraged. As we have explored, the effect of leverage is to increase the return on equity for shareholders, as long as an interest coverage rate of around seven times is preserved. Suppressing the amount of debt simply lowers returns. It also means that the firm will often underinvest in growth. While most firms will only add cost once revenue has been won, it is pretty hard to win many pitches if you haven't got the people to pitch in the first place!

The usual reason for lack of leverage is a failure to understand what it does for shareholders and an absence of specialist debt providers to businesses such as PSFs without fixed assets to act as security. Most banks are keen either for personal guarantees or for corporate assets against which to secure debt. In PSFs there isn't much except for two legged assets! As a result, it shouldn't be surprising that the number of LBOs in the PSF sector is deplorably low compared to the number in industrial businesses.

The other key ingredient missing in many PSFs is committed equity investment. The equity pile tends to be composed mainly of retained earnings, with little external equity participation. The result is that debt-free growth is tough to achieve unless at a painfully slow pace. The time most PSFs need a capital infusion is to make the leap from tier 2 to tier 3 firms.[1] Typically, at this stage they need to add costs faster than they can add revenue and may be involved in small acquisitions. Since few venture funds specialize in PSFs or understand their development process, more aggressive growth firms tend to be forced into the hands of a larger trade buyer who can act as a financier. Trade buyers can offer very positive contributions. If they are a good fit with the ambitions of the PSF, they may be able to offer referrals and an existing network to help it grow internationally. They will also bring financial expertise. But all too often trade investors will come along at a point in a PSF's life cycle when the smaller firm is not in a good negotiating position. Undercapitalization carries a heavy cost!

The usual strategy of a trade investor is to take a minority stake initially which would appear innocuous enough. But such a stake will usually carry minority rights[2] and effectively block any other potential acquirer in the future. They will then be able to extend their share holding at a discount to the real market value as time goes by. The price for access to trade capital and to a network is often selling the farm at a knockdown price!

Were decent PSFs to have access to third-party equity in their development cycle, they would usually be far better positioned to negotiate a healthy market price with trade buyers further down the road or else seek a public listing. Unfortunately, there aren't many third-party investors specializing in the PSF industry. Also, trade buyers usually enjoy a major advantage in pric-

---

[1] See Chapter 2.
[2] Minority rights typically grant a minority shareholder a set of rights to protect their shareholding interest such as blocking issuance of new shares which will dilute their interests or the option of first refusal on new share issues and the ability to block takeover or merger.

ing acquisitions not available to financial investors—they can leverage the existing client relationships of the target and its intellectual products through their own networks. They can therefore build an inherent valuation premium into any deal that keeps many financial investors out.

The venture capital industry has begun to get more active in the PSF area. Europe's largest fund, 3i, and a number of other players are beginning to forge a specialty in the area, recognizing its undercapitalized potential. A number of the US banks have also taken positions in PSFs. The problem facing nonspecialized equity funds is that PSFs are not your average sort of company— the managers tend to be interested in creative quality, market reputation and life style rather than the bottom line. They also tend to lack the quality of financial control of industrials. The business can be dependent on the quality of a finite number of client relationships which PSF professionals will guard from interference. The result is that exerting control as an external shareholder is typically a real challenge, as even the great "Sage of Omaha"[3] found with Salomon Brothers. It is not uncommon for a fund manager to be left with one PSF among a portfolio of industrials, watching the CEO focus on revenue growth with absolutely no uplift in the margins of the business. Unless they know the industry well, their ability to insist on corrective action is limited.

The real underlying problem is that the capital markets themselves are not attuned to the unique qualities of most PSFs. PSFs are driven by people, not capital. They produce customized, intangible products and the entire client business is driven off relationships. This does not mean that there is less potential value in PSFs—structurally there is more than in any other sector. It just means that investing successfully in the sector requires a highly specialized approach. So far in the evolution of the PSF industry virtually no financial institutions have appeared which are geared to cater to the peculiar needs and opportunities of PSFs. There are also only a handful of minor consulting firms that focus on helping companies in the sector. The outcome is simple—trade buyers are the only ones who clearly understand how to invest in PSFs and how to extract

[3] Warren Buffett.

value from them. The result is an industry of the brightest and best 17% of the working population with collective revenues in excess of around $700 billion which lies largely outside the ambit of the capital markets.

WHAT KEEPS POTENTIAL INVESTORS AWAKE AT NIGHT?

As with any other sector, an acquirer will be fundamentally motivated by the target's ability to drop cash to the bottom line—that is, its free cash flow as a percentage of revenue. This will focus attention on the firm's operating profits after tax. Investors tend to look at operating profit after tax in order to exclude the impact of interest income and expense, since they will be concerned with the operating performance of the firm and not with the effects of its capital structure which they will almost certainly change after acquisition. If operating margins are low this will indicate either problems or opportunities. They will also be concerned about the ability of the firm to grow operating profits over time. Historical revenue growth and operating margin performance are usually taken as the best indicator of likely future performance. The absolute margin performance of a PSF is something of a red herring. It gives no indication of sustainability. Above all things, investors are highly sensitized to the quality and durability of the target's earnings.

Most importantly a good acquirer will focus on the firm's dependency on key clients and on key professionals. The greater the client concentration, and hence dependency, the greater will be the discount for risk. Some more sophisticated buyers will audit the reported profits by client and assignment. Undue client dependency will also clearly increase the risk that growth will not materialize. Acquirers will usually begin to get worried if three or less clients account for more than 50% of revenues. Any exposure this generates will be offset in both the structure and timing of payments for the target made by the investor.

If there is heavy client dependence there will also typically be heavy professional dependence. A PSF might have two or three rain makers who hold all the key client relationships even though the firm employs a large number of doers. The loss of these people before adequate succession has been organized can strip the guts out of a business within months, leaving the acquirer with nothing but a brand name.

Because of the peculiar risk profile of PSFs on both the client side and professional side, most trade buyers either buy into targets on an incremental basis or structure the payment schedule around a series of deferred payments based on future performance. The objective is to limit the exposure to systematic PSF risk. In this sense, M&A in the PSF sector differs significantly from its counterpart in the industrial arena where it is common to see firms bought 100% at closing for a single upfront payment.

The other big difference is in the legal documentation surrounding most PSF deals. In PSF deals the focus is on tying professionals in for as long as possible, through non-compete and non-solicit covenants[4] as well as service contracts.[5] Typically, these will prevent principals from operating in the industry for two years after the end of a deal should they leave the acquirer firm. The deferred payment structure of most PSF deals is also geared to tying in key manager shareholders, typically for between a three- and a five-year period. In an important sense, investments in PSFs are geared more at motivating and retaining managers than they are at valuing current assets. The focus of good deals is on incentivizing managers to perform in the future rather than paying them for previous performance or for the assets on the balance sheet of the PSF.

INVESTMENT STRATEGIES AND PRICING

The two most common forms of buy-out or investment in the PSF sector are the "creeping minority" and the "earn-out". Both are structured to limit the commitment of capital before management have guaranteed a viable profit stream for the acquirer going forward.

---

[4] Non-compete and non-solicit covenants ensure that, should a principal leave the acquired firm, he or she will be barred from hiring away employees or from setting up a business which directly competes with the firm in question for a certain period of time.

[5] Service contracts typically specify the amount of notice that must be given either side as well as containing non-solicit and non-compete clauses that largely mirror those in a sale and purchase contract.

The creeping minority

The creeping minority consists of an acquirer taking a minority position in another firm and gradually increasing this minority over time. While a minority position can range up to 49%, it is more common to see an initial position around 25–30%. This acts as a piece of cement tying the two firms together. For the acquirer it serves a particularly useful purpose—it allows it to get a taste of working with the firm in question and to better understand what value it can potentially create. It also ties in the target as both clients and professionals move between the two firms. While the vendor may have the impression that they are maintaining their independence, it is usually the case that the acquirer will gradually get its talons in and extend its shareholding cheaply. The acquirer will also tend to have minority shareholder protection which will allow it to match a bid made on additional shares by any third party or to subscribe for the issuance of any new shares. It will also grant it certain rights over influencing the management of the firm. It is usually the case that the significant presence of a larger PSF in a smaller firm is viewed as a poison pill for any third-party potential investor.

The key issue for the vendor is whether the minority is closed or left hanging. Sometimes larger acquirers will be happy to stay in a firm with an "innocent" minority with no apparent closure mechanism on the remaining shares such as a put or call option. They will then make further purchases when they believe their negotiating position is strongest (for example, after a major client has been referred to the target). If the vendor is sharp they will avoid such open-ended positions in their firms.

The most prevalent method of closing off positions is to sell a minority with a series of options over the remaining shares. Usually these options will be structured as equal-sided puts and calls that allow the seller to put all or part of the remaining shareholding to the buyer at a given point in time based on a preset pricing formula, or for the purchaser to call them. These options are often rolling in nature, renewed annually in the event that neither side chooses to exercise. Typically, both sides will have to notify the other a couple of years before their intention to exercise two years hence in order to provide time to secure the future management of the target. The sensible vendor will tend to look for the exercise of options over 100% of the firm within five years. If, for example, one PSF buys 30% of another at closing for a fixed sum, it might agree to extend its shareholding to a majority of 51% two years hence and then structure a two-sided option over the remaining 49% exercisable five years out (Figure 8.1).

The pricing formula is usually expressed as a multiple of after-tax earnings. As regards the initial interest of 30% in our example, the acquirer will pay a multiple of the firm's after-tax profits times the percentage of the firm's shares being bought. The multiple is a forward multiple—that is, it reflects expectations concerning the future earnings potential of the company. The issue is how to derive the multiple. The capitalized value of any firm is equivalent to its after-tax profits times a multiple.[6] The capitalization represents the cumulative value of its future cash flows discounted back to their net present value.[7] The multiple is simply the inverse or reciprocal of the discount rate, adjusted for growth.[8] Multiples are widely used in PSF deals rather than cash flow valuations because they are simple and because earnings and cash are pretty similar in most PSFs, as we have explored.

The easiest way of deriving a multiple is simply dividing the market value of a quoted comparable firm by its after-tax earnings or, alternatively, by dividing its share price by its earnings per share. The problem with using quoted multiples for private purchases is that they tend to include a large premium for the firm being publicly listed. A quoted firm will often have major PSF brands with strong cash flows, it will be financially sophisticated and have a track record with the investor community. In

---

[6] This capitalized value is the value of all the shares. This differs from enterprise value which would include the value of debt on the balance sheet, less the value of excess cash on the balance sheet.

[7] The calculation of a firm's net present value is illustrated in Figure 8.9. The net present value of a firm should correspond to the collective value of its shares in the market since this is the cash value shareholders can expect to receive in the future as a result of holding their shares.

[8] The calculation of a firm's discount rate is fairly complex and beyond the scope of this book. It reflects the capital structure of the firm and therefore the risk attaching to its shares. The discount rate is used to discount future cash flows to their present value, just as a multiple is used to estimate the total value of future cash flows based on a firm's latest full-year numbers. The multiple and discount rate are therefore the mirror-image of each other.

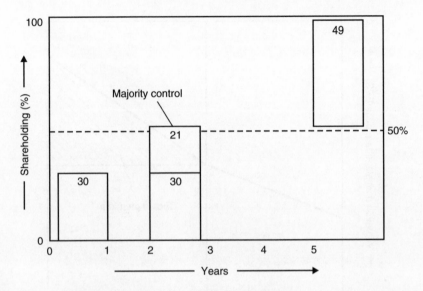

Figure 8.1 *Illustrative shareholding structure of a creeping interest transaction in a PSF*

short, it will be very different from the smaller, private PSF. Therefore the multiples used to buy private firms tend to be heavily discounted from those of their public counterparts. A large conglomerate such as Omnicom, for example, might typically trade at 25 times earnings. Such a firm would begin to squirm if it paid more than 10 times earnings when buying a small private PSF. The difference represents a discount for illiquidity and risk (Figure 8.2). In any particular market it is usually pretty well known at any given point in time what are the upper and lower limits for multiples for different types of firms, depending on their size.

Many vendors get hooked on the multiple used. It, of course, means nothing alone. It depends how and when it is applied to the firm's earnings. The after-tax profits number used for the multiple is as important as the multiple itself. After-tax earnings can be played around with in a number of ways which will significantly affect the resulting valuation.

First, the sophisticated buyer will tend to use the operating profits after tax or OPAT rather than the straight profit after-tax

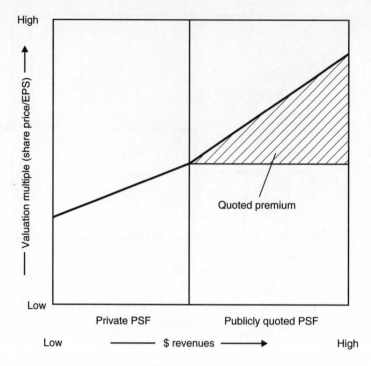

Figure 8.2   *Illustrative relationship between valuation multiples and financial status of a typical PSF*

number or PAT. It makes no sense for a firm to pay for a multiple of interest earnings which are dependent on its cash pile and handling of passthrough cash balances and not its operating ability. For PSFs with little debt and lots of passthrough costs this can be a large number. If an acquirer uses OPAT for purposes of calculation, it will then deduct off any debt in the company from the resulting valuation (and add any excess cash on the balance sheet to the purchase price). Debt is owed to lenders and there-fore has to be paid out of the value of the firm.

A sophisticated vendor will, in turn, usually add back excep-tional items such as the cost to move building or the firing of a senior executive which are unlikely to be regularly recurring costs. The effect of such adjustments will be to increase the reported profits after tax of the firm. They may also release accruals and reserves to boost revenue as well as exploiting the timing of cost and revenue recognition (particularly with WIP) to

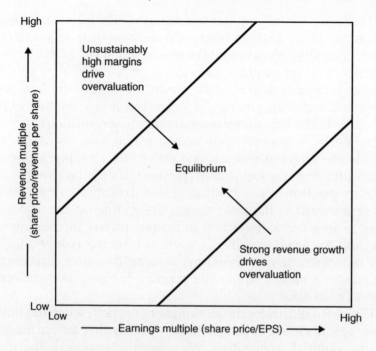

Figure 8.3 *Illustrative relationship between earnings multiples and revenue multiples in a PSF*

inflate reported earnings for the purposes of a buy-out calculation period.[9] This will clearly be determined by the sophistication and amenability of their auditors who have to sign off on the accounts.

Conversely, buyers will be alert to inflated margins which may not be sustainable. The usual way to see whether unsustainable margins are jacking up the purchase price is to check the revenue multiple (the valuation price divided by revenue or gross margin). If this multiple is high, say in excess of three times, then it is fairly sure that the firm's margins are too high to be sustainable. The revenue multiple and the earnings multiple should be in equilibrium. If they are not, then something is wrong with the basis of valuation as a result of an excessively low or high margin (Figure 8.3).

---

[9] This should show up in large increases in receivables and sharp drops in WIP as well as an increase in the average aged debtor's profile.

The sophisticated acquirer will also typically focus on the issue of salary. Many entrepreneurs will depress their salary drawn from operating profits and take rewards instead in the form of dividends. If an acquirer fails to adjust the executive salaries upwards before calculating the profits after tax of the firm, then they will wind up paying the seller too much relative to the earnings of the firm under normal operating conditions.

Similarly, a sophisticated acquirer will also focus on applying the ongoing real tax rate rather than the particular tax rate of the firm for the year in question. Using the effective tax rate of the firm can introduce major distortions from reality going forward as the rate changes depending on the firm's access to loss carryforwards[10] and other means of creating tax shields. An acquirer will not want to bear the risk of shifting tax outcomes. It will, therefore, assume that there are no tax shields and simply apply the average national rate for companies of its size.

Figure 8.4 illustrates the key adjustments both seller and buyer will typically make in calculating the profits after tax for the firm at the point of acquisition. As already mentioned, the most important will be the treatment of interest expense and therefore debt. If interest expense is left in calculating PAT, debt cannot be deducted off the consideration since this would be double-counting. The same is true of interest income and cash. If interest income is left in, then the acquirer should keep all excess cash rather than dividending it out since they will be paying for the value of that cash.[11]

Of course, the key is not simply the financials for the year in question. It is the sustainability of performance in the years going forward. What is the volume of repeat business? How much income is on a retainer basis? How fundamentally attractive is the client base? In PSF deals the future is what matters. The key for the acquirer is that they don't want to buy on the basis of past performance, but rather on future potential. Historical numbers are a guide but not a guarantee.

---

[10] Loss carryforwards are reported losses which can be brought forward from prior years to act as tax shields against positive net income in the current year.

[11] Most vendors will try to dividend out as much cash as possible before a deal has been agreed in order to prevent it being left stranded in the company they no longer control. For the buyer, it is essential that, if this has happened, the firm does not get credited for interest income on cash it no longer has on the balance sheet.

Proforma P & L		Adjustments	
Billings	1000		
Revenue	500		
Staff costs	(280) ⟶	Adjust director ⟶	(300)
		salaries to market	
Overhead	(100)		
Operating profit	120		100
Exceptional items	(30) ①⟶	Add back exceptionals ⟶	30
Interest received	20 ⟶	Ignore ⟶	0 ③
Interest paid	(15) ⟶	Ignore ⟶	0
Profit before tax	125		130
Tax	(20) ⟶	Normalize ⟶	(45)
Profit after tax	75		85
Dividends to directors	(50)		—
Retained earnings	45		85 ②

① Deducted from operating profit (includes provisions, write-offs, one-off expenses and income, etc.)

② = operating profit after tax or OPAT

③ Assumes debt deducted off valuation of equity and excess cash dividended out to vendors

Figure 8.4 *Illustration of typical adjustments to the P&L of a PSF during the process of valuation*

In our illustrative structure, therefore, the payments for the second and third tranche of shares are usually made contingent on future growth rates. If growth rates are high it is more likely that the firm will continue to create incremental value going forward. This expectation will be reflected in a higher multiple. As a result, a firm growing at 20% will command a higher multiple than one growing at only 10%. Growth rates and the value placed on a firm are tightly correlated because the higher the growth, the greater the potential profits that will be produced in the future for shareholders.

Revenue growth is not the key issue in and of itself. What matters is growth in after-tax profits (as a close proxy for cash flow in PSFs), although obviously this can only come with good revenue growth. The multiple applied to the payment in year 3, in our example, will usually be made to depend on the compound annual growth rate ('cagr') from year 0 through to the end of year 3 and the option payment in year 5 will be dependent on the five-year cagr. Figure 8.5 illustrates a set of multiples and their relationship with growth over the period. Growth is usually measured by buyers in terms of after-tax profits (either PAT or OPAT), not operating profits, to fully reflect the risks associated with any changes in tax rates.

Although widely used, the cagr is actually not always the most accurate measure for an acquirer, for it does not require a PSF to hit certain growth targets each year, just a mathematical average

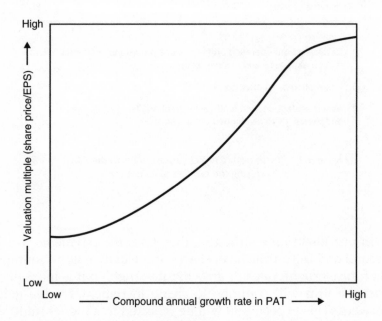

Figure 8.5   *Illustrative relationship between valuation multiples and growth rates for a PSF*

over the entire period. As a result, acquirers will often specify minimum earnings numbers or hurdles that must be achieved each year to insulate themselves against undue volatility in earnings.

In terms of the PAT or OPAT number used for the calculation, sophisticated acquirers will typically use an average number for the period of the deal. In our example, this might mean an average of the PATs for years 0 to 3 for the second payment and then the average of the PATs for years 1 to 5 for the third payment. The use of an average PAT number obviously has the effect of dampening the exit multiple[12] for the acquirer. But it also has the effect of creating an incentive for the vendor management to maximize growth in earnings each year over the entire period. Figure 8.6 illustrates the typical structure of a creeping interest deal.

Earn-outs

The main alternative to the creeping interest purchase strategy is the "earn-out". Under an earn-out the acquirer takes 100% of the share capital of the target upfront in return for a set of deferred payments, typically over five years. The deferred payments are usually determined in much the same way as with the creeping interest structure. The multiples are driven by the compound annual growth in after-tax earnings over the period.

The usual difference between the creeping interest and the earn-out structure is that the multiples are increased during the course of the earn-out period on a sliding scale. As the illustrative structure laid out in Figure 8.7 shows, the key for the acquirer is to leave enough value on the table to keep the vendor engaged enough to grow the business over the earn-out period. Therefore, the ramping-up of multiples is used to ensure that there will be plenty to aim for in addition to the initial payment.

The creeping interest and earn-out structures can be calibrated to release the same payment to the vendor, with roughly the same scheduling of payments at an average growth rate. The

---

[12] The exit multiple is the total price paid for an acquisition divided by the after tax earnings of the firm in the last year of the earn-out or when the final payment is made.

Multiple: Growth in OPAT (or PAT)   Year 0 as base

0 – 10%	5 x
11 – 20%	7 x
21 – 30%	9 x
31% +	10 x

Payments: Year

0	5 x year 0 OPAT x 30%	
2	5,7,9 or 10 x average OPAT (year 0,1,2)	x 21%
5	5,7,9 or 10 x average OPAT (year 1–5)	x 49%

Cashflow example:

Year	0	1	2	3	4	5
OPAT $^{\circledast}$	100	110	121	133	146	161
Payment	70		116			329
Debt	50					
Excess cash	10					
Cumulative net payments	30		146			475
Unadjusted exit multiple						3 x

$\circledast$ CAGR = 10%

Figure 8.6 *Illustrative structure of a typical creeping interest transaction in a PSF*

difference in the two structures occurs at either end of the growth spectrum. In a situation where future growth is likely to be spectacular, a buyer will be better off with a creeping acquisition. The upfront purchase of a fixed share means that the vendor will not be fully credited with the increase in profits. The earn-out, by comparison, leaves the vendor with full exposure to the upside (although absolute payments will usually be capped at an agreed amount, limiting their upside exposure). When it comes to the downside the opposite is true. In a creeping interest situation a buyer will have bought a share at a fixed price which may bear no relation to the value of the rest of the stock going forward if circumstances change. They will therefore share this risk with

Multiple: Growth in OPAT (or PAT)   Year 0 as base

0 – 10%	5 x
11 – 20%	7 x
21 – 30%	9 x
30% +	10 x

Payments: Year

0	5 x OPAT year 0
1	5 x average OPAT year (0,1) – payment 1
2	5 or 7 x average OPAT year (0,1,2) – payments 1,2
3	5 or 7 x average OPAT year (0,1,2,3) – payments 1,2,3
4	5,7 or 9 x average OPAT year (0–4) – payments 1–4
5	5,7,9 or 10 x average OPAT year (0–5) – payments 1–5

Cashflow example:

Year	0	1	2	3	4	5
OPAT ⊛	100	110	121	133	146	161
Payment	500	25	27	28	30	32
Debt	(50)					
Excess cash	10					
Cumulative net payments	460	485	512	540	570	602
Unadjusted exit multiple						4 x

⊛ CAGR = 10%

Figure 8.7 *Illustrative structure of a typical earn-out transaction in a PSF*

the vendor. In the earn-out, the exposure is typically lower as the vendor will still be fully exposed to the downside risk, reducing the payment they receive accordingly. Figure 8.8 compares the distinct risk profiles of the two structures.

The result of the different risk profiles of the two structures is that sophisticated buyers will usually go for earn-outs. Risks are lower and managers will be more incentivized to grow the bottom line. Earn-outs have the additional benefit to buyers that they will own 100% of the stock from day one and can therefore fully consolidate the earnings and revenues. As well as boosting

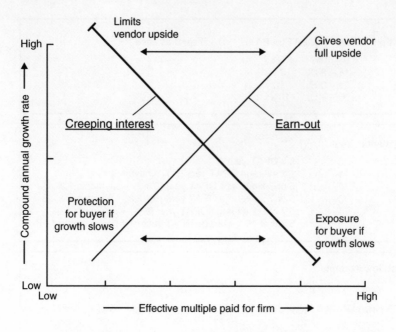

Figure 8.8   *Illustrative comparison of the risk profiles of earn-outs versus creeping interest acquisitions*

the reported profits of the acquirer from day one of the acquisition, this also means they can implement tax-pooling strategies. There is also the issue of dividends. In a creeping acquisition the vendor still has a claim on annual dividends equivalent to its share of the firm's stock. In an earn-out, since the buyer holds 100%, all dividends flow to the buyer from closing. These can be significant and help the deal pay for itself, shortening the payback period. Vendors rarely factor this lost cash flow into the deals they negotiate.

In contrast to sophisticated buyers, vendors typically opt for incremental sell-outs, usually not for economically rational reasons but simply because they fear losing full control from the outset. As we have already explored, this is all somewhat self-deluding since the acquirer will typically extend from its minority position under advantageous pricing arrangements.

In both dominant acquisition structures, net debt (after netting out of excess cash above working capital needs), including any preference shares, is deducted from the capitalized value of the firm. The full acquisition price, or "enterprise value", is the sum of the debt and the net valuation of the equity less excess cash left on the balance sheet. Both structures on paper look pretty much awash. But in PSF valuation methodology this is not the primary issue. The key question is, which method of paying best incentivizes the vendor management to perform going forward in the particular situation of the firm in question?

PULLING IT ALL TOGETHER

Interestingly, neither valuation approach bears any relation to the balance sheet assets of the company or its book value. Most PSF acquirers get uncomfortable with very low or negative net assets because this limits their ability to draw out dividends in the future, and because it may reflect poor underlying salaries which have been supplemented with full dividends in the past. However, they will not refer to the asset base of the company in determining pricing. The only real balance sheet concern will be the current asset position, which reflects the firm's cash flow situation, and its debt position. Otherwise the balance sheet is largely irrelevant to pricing.

The other difference between PSF valuation and industrial valuation is the issue of cash flow. Nowadays, most larger industrial valuations are done on the basis of discounted cash flow valuations or DCFs. A generic DCF calculation for a five-year period is illustrated in Figure 8.9. All that matters for the acquirer is how much free cash the business will throw off going forward and the net present value of these cash flows. The calculation of free cash flow requires adjustments to the after-tax profits of the business for non-cash items such as depreciation and for capital consuming items such as the change in net current assets and capex (Figure 8.10). These flows are then discounted at the cost of capital of the firm—a blend of the cost of debt and the expected return on the equity given the risk of the investment.

By contrast, in the case of most PCFs there is not much difference between profit and cash flow. PSFs don't have much capital to depreciate, and have low capex requirements. In the absence of major office moves and depreciated refits, profits are a good

Year $m	0	1	2	3	4	5
Cash flow	100	110	120	130	140	150
Discount rate ①	1	1.15^1	1.15^2	1.15^3	1.15^4	1.15^5
Discount factor	0	1.15	1.32	1.52	1.75	2.01
Perpetuity ②				((150 X 1.05)/0.15)$/1.15^5$		
Present value	100	95.7	90.9	85.5	80	597
Net debt	200					
NPV	849					

① Assumes discount rate of 15%

② Assuming 5% growth rate into the future

Figure 8.9   *Illustrative calculation of NPV for a PSF*

indicator of cash flow. The only substantial adjustment is any shift in net working capital requirements and since PSFs tend to have low reserves, they tend not to accumulate large positive working capital balances. The result is that profit and cash are virtually the same thing, which makes life simple.

PSFs also differ from most industrials in the simplicity of their liabilities. Apart from overdraft facilities, it tends to be all equity. If you take the standard unleveraged rate of return (which will assume there is no risk resulting from leverage in the balance sheet) for the sector and subtract the anticipated growth rate, then you have the discount rate for a PSF for purposes of calculating a perpetuity. This makes the multiple (which, as we have explored, is a reciprocal of the discount rate) a fairly reliable tool in place of the complex discount rate formulas used for valuing cash flows in most industrials.

PSF valuation is a simple process. The key to structuring a good deal is to motivate management to perform. They are the

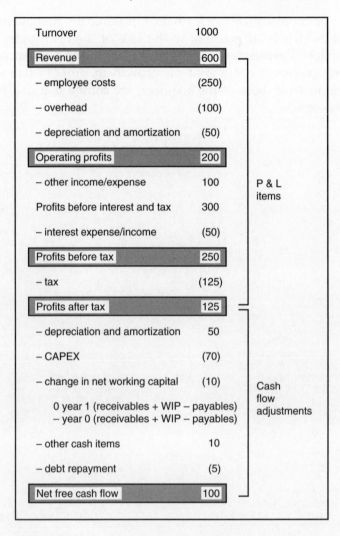

Turnover	1000
Revenue	600
– employee costs	(250)
– overhead	(100)
– depreciation and amortization	(50)
Operating profits	200
– other income/expense	100
Profits before interest and tax	300
– interest expense/income	(50)
Profits before tax	250
– tax	(125)
Profits after tax	125
– depreciation and amortization	50
– CAPEX	(70)
– change in net working capital	(10)
0 year 1 (receivables + WIP – payables) – year 0 (receivables + WIP – payables)	
– other cash items	10
– debt repayment	(5)
Net free cash flow	100

P & L items

Cash flow adjustments

Figure 8.10 *Illustrative reconciliation of reported profits and free cash flow in a PSF*

only reliable asset you are buying! All the future equity lies in professional motivation and the client relationships it creates. Therefore a structure is as good as its ability to inspire great deeds. It is because of this that all intelligent PSF pricing structures focus rewards on future performance and growth in earnings, not on historical performance, linking the management's future as closely as possible to the fate of the firm under new ownership. Payments in shares of the acquiring company, and making payment contingent on growth in profits of the firm combined with those of the acquirer, are common added twists of the screw.

9
The Future for
Professional Service Firms

The global professional service sector is set to become one of the star growth performers of the next decade. It has been a silent, fragmented star for the past decade, hidden in the balance sheets of privately held firms. Composed of a vast collection of small, specialist firms at one end and a few large quoted conglomerates at the other, it has attracted little attention. Consultants tend not to study themselves! Yet it has consistently sucked brainpower away from the mature industrials and gathered it into groups of like-minded people. Through this process it is progressively winning control of the knowledge and knowhow of client companies. And it is these intangible assets which are now recognized as the key asset of most firms (even if they do not appear on the balance sheet).

In addition to their focus on knowledge management, PSFs have mastered the ability to manage and motivate extremely bright people. These two features, the management of talent and knowledge, make the PSF sector the model for the rest of industry over the next twenty years. It has taken the concept of value-added to the extreme and stripped away all non-essential material assets. As a result, it is able to produce a return on equity far in excess of that of any asset-driven business. As clients become more and more dependent on PSFs to help them add value to their products and services, so these returns will increase. The industrial world will polarize into firms that manage capital and material goods and those that manage and apply raw talent and knowledge. It is clear where the winners will lie!

The obscurity of the PSF sector will not last. Already, firms such as McKinsey, Goldman Sachs and Arthur Andersen are beginning to be raised as benchmarks for value management. The problem is that managers and academics don't know much about them or the way they work. As a long line of smaller PSFs begin to come to market for capital for expansion and acquisitions this will begin to change. Their economics will be better understood and their role in the new information-led economy better exposed.

So if that's the big picture, what's happening at ground level? Things are moving fast. First, at a time when many traditional industries in the mature economies of the West are retrenching in the face of the low-cost East and grappling for sources of competitive advantage, the PSF sector continues to show spectacular growth, in aggregate around the 20% mark. Why? Industrials have basically made the irreversible decision to outsource many of their thinking functions, from competitor intelligence to tax structuring. As fast as these industrials are shedding skilled labour, the PSF industry is picking it up. At the same time the need for industrial and service companies to move away from production-led strategies to product and service innovation-led strategies is becoming inexorable. They increasingly have to excel in inventiveness, in their understanding of their customers and in their ability to market to them effectively—all functions now provided by PSFs. These two forces—outsourcing and the shift to intangibles as a basis of competitive advantage—will ensure high levels of growth for PSFs even in the mature economies of the West. The same cannot be said for many other areas of activity!

Second, there is an unstoppable push for internationalization by most PSFs on the coat-tails of their major clients. Firms which have not yet established an organic network *à la* McKinsey are being forced to speed up their pace of expansion through acquisition. This is driving their need for capital. As the number of these larger networks increases, so too will the opportunities for small private PSFs to grow their business organically and then sell out to consolidated networks. The volume of M&A and market listings will increase rapidly over the next ten years. With it will grow investor interest.

The third major trend is the dual tension between increasing specialization as PSF sectors mature and the push for bundling and integration by larger groups. The past ten years have seen a rapid crystallization of different lines of specialty service. In the marketing services world, healthcare advertising is now viewed as a quite separate discipline from database direct marketing or sports sponsorship. In the world of consulting, BPR work is viewed as quite distinct from competitor intelligence work. This process of segmentation and specialization is the natural byproduct of the maturation of any service. On the other side of the equation there are the larger PSF groups whose principal objective is to dominate global client groups by providing integrated solutions. A McCann-Erickson servicing a client such as General Motors doesn't want to see its advertising offering undercut by another competitor touting promotional devices. So they buy them. This process of flanking among PSFs is endemic. The justification is synergy and often this is a quite legitimate reason. The two counterforces of integration and specialization will ensure a decade or more of turmoil and reshuffling.

Fourth, there will persist the related tension between consolidation and fragmentation. In most industries the trend is in one direction only, as producers consolidate to achieve the scale to compete on a global basis. As a result, most sectors have seen the number of significant global competitors shrink to a handful of players. In areas such as global aircraft manufacturing there are basically only two left. The PSF sector has seen a similar process of consolidation, with firms such as the Big Six dominating the global accountancy world and the BCGs and McKinseys controlling the strategy industry. The same is true in sectors as diverse as legal advisory and investment banking.

However, consolidation in the PSF arena is primarily an issue when it comes to servicing the finite number of clients that qualify as global. As a percentage of total spend in most PSF sectors, this remains a minority of the overall business. The majority of it in terms of revenue is still associated with regional or national accounts and these tend to be serviced most attentively by multi-local networks or smaller, more focused PSFs in national and regional markets. The net effect will be continued diversity, lots of activity and a natural dynamic between large and smaller firms.

Right now, the PSF industry does not exist. PSFs are lumped into industrial sectors such as Media, Finance, General Services, etc. Of course, as we have explored in this short book, the diverse range of PSF firms have much more in common with each other than they do with the notional areas of business activity with which they are commonly classified. The PSF industry is, in many ways, waiting to be invented.

Select Bibliography

There are surprisingly few books which focus on the business issues faced in the PSF industry despite its enormous size. The following are some of the better books that touch upon the various issues commonly confronted in the PSF industry, although only a few of them focus specifically on PSFs themselves.

Buzell, R. D. and Gale, B. T. (1987). *The PIMS Principles: Linking Strategy to Performance*. The Free Press.

Camp, R. C. (1989) *Benchmarking: The Search for Industry Best Practices that Lead to Superior Performance*. Quality Press.

Campbell, A. Goold, M. and Alexander, M. (1994). *Corporate Level Strategy: Creating Value in the Multi-Business Company*. John Wiley.

Champy, J. (1995). *Reengineering Management: The Mandate for New Leadership*. Harper Business.

Copeland, T. and Koller, T. (1994). *Valuation: Measuring and Managing the Value of Companies*, 2nd edition. John Wiley.

Creech, B. (1994). *The Five Pillars of TQM: How to Make TQM Work for You*. Dutton.

Davidson, B. and Davis, S. (1991). *2020 Vision: Transforming Your Business Today To Succeed Tomorrow*. Simon & Schuster.

Davis, S. (1987). *Future Perfect*. Addison-Wesley.

Hamel, G. and Prahalad, C. K. (1984). Competing for the Future. *Harvard Business Review*, August.

Hamel, G. and Prahalad, C. K. (1994). *Competing for the Future: Breakthrough Strategies for Seizing Control*. Harvard Business School Press.

Hammer, M. (1995). *Beyond Reengineering*. Harper Business.

Hammer, M. and Champy, J. (1994). *Reengineering the Corporation: A Manifesto for Business Revolution*. Harper Business.

Hampden-Turner, C. (1992). *Creating Corporate Culture: From Discord to Harmony*. Addison-Wesley.

Hart, C. W. L., Heskett J. L. and Sasser, E. W., Jr (1990). The Profitable Art of Service Recovery. *Harvard Business Review*, July/August.

Heskett, J. L., Jones, T. O., Loveman, G., Sasser E. W., Jr and Schlesinger, L. A. (1994). Putting the Service Profit Chain to Work. *Harvard Business Review*, March/April.

Heskett, J. L., Sasser, E. W., Jr. and Hart, C. W. L. (1990). *Service Breakthroughs: Changing the Rules of the Game*. The Free Press.

Kanter, R. M. (1994) Collaborative Advantage: the Art of Alliances. *Harvard Business Review*, July/August.

Kaplan, R. S. and Norton, D. P. (1993). Putting the Balanced Scorecard to Work. *Harvard Business Review*, September/October.

Katzenbach, J. and Smith, D. (1993). *The Wisdom of Teams*, Harvard Business School Press.

Kohn, A. (1993). Why Incentive Plans Cannot Work. *Harvard Business Review*, September/October.

Kotler, P. (1989). From Mass Marketing to Mass Customization. *Planning Review*, September/October.

Kotter, J. and Heskett, J. (1992). *Corporate Culture and Performance*. The Free Press.

Kotter, J. P. (1995). Leading Change: Why Transformation Efforts Fail. *Harvard Business Review*, March/April.

Larkin, T. J. (1994) *Communicating Change*. McGraw-Hill.

Lowendahl, Bente Strategic Management of Professional Service Firms. Copenhagen Business School Press, 1997.

Maister, D. (1994). *Managing the Professional Service Firm*. The Free Press.

Maister, D. (1997). *True Professionalism*. The Free Press.

Meyer, C. (1994). How the Right Measures Help Teams Excel. *Harvard Business Review*, May/June.

Millar, V. *On the Management of Professional Service Firms*. Kennedy Publications, 1991.

Mohrman, S. A., Cohen, S. G. and Mohrman, A. M. (1995). *Designing Team-Based Organizations: New Forms of Knowledge Work*. Jossey-Bass.

Nonaka, I. and Takeuchi, H. (1995). *The Knowledge Creating Company: How Japanese Companies Create the Dynamics of Innovation*. Oxford University Press.

Ostroff, F. and Smith, D. (1992). The Horizontal Organization: Redesigning the Corporation. *The McKinsey Quarterly*, No. 1.

Peppers, D. and Rogers, M. (1995). A New Marketing Paradigm: Share of Customer not Market Share. *Planning Review*. March/April.

Peppers, D. and Rogers, M. (1993). *The One to One Future: Building Relationships One at a Time*. Currency Doubleday.

Pine. B. J., II (1992). *Mass Customization.* Harvard Business School Press.

Pine, B. J., II, Peppers, D. and Rogers, M. (1995). Do You Want to Keep Your Customers for Ever? *Harvard Business Review*, March/April.

Porass, J. J. and Collins, J. C. (1994). *Built to Last: Successful Habits of Visionary Companies.* Harper Business.

Porter, M. E. (1980). *Competitive Strategy. Techniques for Analyzing Industries and Competitors.* The Free Press.

Porter, M. E. (1985). *Competitive Advantage: Creating and Sustaining Superior Performance.* The Free Press.

Porter, M. E. (1987). From Competitive Advantage to Corporate Strategy. *Harvard Business Review*, March.

Poynter, T. A. and White, R. E. (1990). Making the Horizontal Organization Work. *Business Quarterly*, Winter.

Prahalad, C. K. and Hamel, G. (1990). The Core Competencies of the Corporation. *Harvard Business Review*, May/June.

Rappaport, A. (1986) *Creating Shareholder Value: A New Standard for Business.* The Free Press.

Ray, D. W. and Bronstein, H. (1995). *Teaming Up: Making the Transition to a Self Directed, Team-based Organization.* McGraw-Hill.

Reichheld, F. F. (1993). Loyalty Based Management. *Harvard Business Review*, March/April.

Risher, H. and Fay, C. (1995). *The Performance Imperative: Strategies for Enhancing Workforce Effectiveness.* Jossey-Bass.

Schlesinger, L. A. and Heskett, J. L. (1991). The Service-Driven Service Company. *The Harvard Business Review*, September/October.

Scott, M. C. (1998). *Value Drivers: The Manager's Framework for Identifying the Drivers of Corporate Value Creation.* John Wiley.

Stalk, G., Evans, P. and Schulman, L. E. (1992). Competing on Capabilities: The New Rules of Corporate Strategy. *Harvard Business Review*, March/April.

Spector, R. A. (1995). *Taking Charge and Letting Go: Breakthrough Strategies for Creating and Managing the Horizontal Company.* The Free Press.

Svelby, K. E. (1997). *The New Organizational Wealth: Managing and Measuring Knowledge-Based Assets.* Berrett Koehler.

Weiss, A. *How to Maximise Fees in Professional Service Firms.* Summit Consulting Group, 1994.

Wellins, R. S., Byham, W. C. and Dixon, G. R. (1994). *Inside Teams: How 20 World Class Organizations are Winning Through Teamwork.* Jossey-Bass.

Index